You're Too Cute to Be Disabled

Living with Limb-Girdle Muscular Dystrophy

Shelley Tudin

iUniverse, Inc.
Bloomington

You're Too Cute to Be Disabled
Living with Limb-Girdle Muscular Dystrophy

iUniverse books may be ordered through booksellers or by contacting:

iUniverse
1663 Liberty Drive
Bloomington, IN 47403
www.iuniverse.com
1-800-Authors (1-800-288-4677)

ISBN: 978-1-4697-3710-2 (sc)
ISBN: 978-1-4697-3711-9 (hc)
ISBN: 978-1-4697-3712-6 (e)

Printed in the United States of America

iUniverse rev. date: 2/13/2012

In memory of my father, who passed away ten years ago. A day does not go by that I can't feel your spirit, your determination, and your courage around me.

When you feel like giving up, remember why you held on for so long in the first place.

—Anonymous online quote

Contents

Acknowledgments

A special thank-you to the most generous woman in my life, my dear mother. She is the strongest, most selfless woman, giving of herself, yet enduring so much.

To my sister, Michele, and my brother, John, who share the same disease, muscular dystrophy, and face each day with courage and hope.

To my friends and family who always believed I could achieve anything I set my mind to.

A special thank-you to my dear friend, Uncle Buck, who had a kind, gentle soul and offered his endless support to my family. We will never forget you.

And to Jeff, my dear, loving husband and best friend. You helped me believe in love again. I could not have accomplished so much without your love and support.

Introduction

Not that my life has been any more exciting or tragic than the next person's, but I have had an interesting life, if I do say so myself. You know the adage: "If shit happens, it happens to me." This phrase pretty much sums up my life.

At the age of eleven, I was diagnosed with limb-girdle muscular dystrophy. During the first few years after my diagnosis, I carried on with my daily routine as if nothing had changed. Certain physical changes were happening to my body. I didn't want to give up certain sporting activities, such as figure skating. Eventually, my muscles began to atrophy. This made the simple tasks of running, walking up and down stairs, and even getting up from a chair difficult to do. As I acknowledged my dream of becoming a champion figure skater was not going to happen, my self-esteem plummeted.

Living with a disability is difficult. So many people look at the outer surface of a person's body and forget the importance of our inner beauty. My life changed in many ways after the diagnosis of muscular dystrophy. I learned how to cope with this disease, continued on with my education, dealt with romantic relationships, found employment, and coped with the loss of relationships and loved ones.

In the early years, tragic events caused me to experience a major depression. Knowing that these negative events could control my life left me feeling completely defeated. After losing some of the most important people in my life, I realized how strong I was. I learned to depend on myself; I didn't need to rely on others to make me feel satisfied or whole.

Life has a way of throwing us a curveball when we least expect it. People say life is a journey, not a destination. Through my life experiences, I have gained confidence, wisdom, and the power of positive thinking to turn my dreams into realities. This story will take you on my journey. As a young, frightened girl, I struggled to cope with my disability. With a lot of love, laughter, and tears, I became a self-confident, happy, independent, and incredibly tenacious woman.

I recently watched an episode of Dr. Phil. He was talking with a group of single women who were involved with married men. These women invested a lot of time with men who were never going to commit to them. He explained that losers stay in the same unhappy situation; winners move forward and make a change. Whatever situation you are in, never let anyone treat you disrespectfully. You are worth more than that.

For the most part, I am one of those people that others like. I'm kind of funny and witty, and I'm a character and, unquestionably, a true leader. My cousin Sue once said to me that I have a mesmerizing personality. People want to hear what I have to say. I never really considered myself as someone special, certainly not anyone famous. Books are usually written about famous people, such as Princess Diana or Martin Luther King. Does anyone really want to read about me, a forty-seven-year-old woman, a talented struggling artist living with a disability? I hope my life experiences will allow others living with muscular dystrophy or other physical disabilities to focus on your personal attributes and not on the limitations that are not within your control.

Muscular dystrophy can steal parts of a person's body strength, but it does not affect a person's intellect, mind, or determination. There is no cure for limb-girdle muscular dystrophy, but research has come a long way in identifying genes and approaching the possibility of one day discovering a cure. Receiving a diagnosis of muscular dystrophy is shocking and scary, but it does not have to be a death sentence. We all have physical differences—the colour of our skin, our body shape, and even our physical limitations. Instead of focusing on our differences, we should focus on our similarities of inner strength, morals, love, and happiness.

This is my true story about living with a disability, overcoming adversity, and living life to the fullest!

Early Childhood

I was raised and still reside in Brantford, Ontario, Canada. It is an average-sized city about one hour southwest of Toronto. Many famous people have come from Brantford, but the two who come to mind are Alexander Graham Bell, inventor of the telephone, and Wayne Gretzky, one of the greatest hockey players of our time.

My childhood was not unusual. My working-class parents raised three children: Michele was the oldest sibling; I, the infamous middle child, was born ten-and-a-half months later in 1964; and my brother, John, was the baby of the family. For those of you who are doing the calculations, my mother went in for her six-week checkup after delivering her first child in September 1963—and learned she was pregnant with me. Maybe that's when my energetic personality and spirited nature began.

As a young child, I was the hyper one and tested my parents whenever I could. Our house on Kensington Avenue was where all the neighbourhood kids hung out. My mother always said that it was such a difficult task getting me to come inside for dinner or bedtime. I would rather wet my pants than take the time to come inside for a bathroom break. Heaven forbid I miss some of the action! Driving to a cottage on summer vacations, Michele sat on one side and Johnny sat on the other, sleeping so calmly. I was the one in the middle and every ten minutes asked, "Are we there yet? How much farther?" I can't remember a time when my parents had private conversations that I didn't hear.

My father used to say, "Nothing gets past this one. Shelley, go to sleep!"

Michele (left), age three, and Shelley (right), age two

While I wasn't quiet at home, I was a shy child in school. Still, I always volunteered at the end of the school year to help the teacher clean her classroom. I guess I was a people pleaser. I always got good grades; some probably called me the teacher's pet. In first grade, I produced a painting of a tree with falling leaves. I remember my teacher commenting to others that it was rare to see a six-year-old child create a three-dimensional landscape. Maybe this was the start of a budding young artist!

As a small child, I never excelled in sports. I loved to figure skate. My parents even paid for private lessons when I entered into our local skating club's competition. I do remember looking at the results later that day. My name was at the bottom of the list, placing thirtieth out of thirty. I don't know if this was supposed to be character building, but something told me that I was not going to be the next Dorothy Hamill.

Every winter, my dad made the biggest ice rink in the neighbourhood. With their skates and hockey sticks, the neighbour kids headed to our backyard. We always picked captains, who then chose their team members one by one. You probably know where this is going: I was always the last child waiting to be selected and relegated to the net. The boys fired the puck so hard at me that I dove out of the way. The sponge pucks stung when they hit my frozen limbs. One thing I hated more than being last was being in pain. Rejection was tough, but I think I got used to it. I may not have had any athletic ability in my tiny frame, but boy did I try.

Limited edition print, Figure Skates by Shelley Tudin

Shelley, age three

I remember those cold, winter evenings when my parents and siblings took turns holding the frigid hose and flooding the rink. Mr. Gretzky, father of the famous hockey player Wayne, lived one block over. He informed my father that using a sprinkler would create the perfect ice surface. Who would have thought flooding a rink with a sprinkler could be so easy, and much warmer? One of us would run outside and move the sprinkler every hour. My mother was concerned the rink was too large because our backyard bordered two large, eight-foot metal clothes line posts cemented into the ground. My mother argued with my father and boldly stated, "John, someone is going to skate into one of those posts and seriously injure himself."

My father replied, "Rosaleen, you worry too much."

One evening, my father played scrimmage hockey with the neighbourhood kids. One of the MacGregor boys passed my father the puck at the edge of the rink. As he skated toward the net on a breakaway, my father suddenly stopped dead as he hit his head on the metal post and fell back on the ice. I am sure he saw stars that evening that were not the real ones that glittered so brilliantly in the dark winter sky. We all watched to see if there was any life or movement from my father lying so still on the ice.

Dad slowly sat up and said, "God, I hate it when Rosaleen is right!"

Everyone laughed hysterically. The boys helped my father stand upright; one of them assisted him off the ice. My father had a wicked headache that night and finally acknowledged that having the biggest skating rink in the neighbourhood was not safe. The following winter, our rink was smaller in size with the edge of the ice ending two feet shy of those metal posts.

The Diagnosis

When I was eleven, my life changed. One day, my father took me to one of my softball games at a park not too far from our home. When it was my turn up to bat, I got a hit and started running to first base. Unbeknownst to me, a young woman sitting beside my father noticed I was having difficulty running as I barely made it to the base. This woman happened to be a nurse. She spoke to my father and asked him to talk to our doctor about the physical difficulties I was having. She definitely thought something was not quite right. My father was a little embarrassed, but he never considered the possibility of the events that were about to follow.

After a visit with our family doctor, he arranged two referrals, one to an allergy specialist and one to an orthopaedic surgeon. A few weeks passed before my mother took me to our local allergy specialist for my appointment. I remember the drive to the doctor's office and my comment to my mother: "I hope I'm allergic to smoke. Dad and you will have to quit smoking."

The doctor called my mom into his office after the allergy test was over. I assumed I had some serious allergies that he wanted to discuss privately with my mom. Unfortunately, I wasn't diagnosed as allergic to smoke, but something else that none of us could have foreseen happened.

My mother left his office with a worried look on her face. What I didn't know at the time was that Dr. Patel noticed a tiny, eleven-year-old girl who got up from a chair in his waiting room—a little girl who put her hand on her leg to push herself up. He also noticed a strange, waddling gait to my walk. Later that week on Dr. Patel's advice, my mother took me to another doctor for a blood test. I remember seeing the orthopaedic surgeon. He had commented about my knee caps being turned in. At that time, the doctors believed I may have swivelled hips. Later in life, after speaking to my mother, she informed me that Dr. Patel asked if our family had a history of muscular dystrophy. My mother was shocked and told him that there was no history of this disease in our family.

I don't remember the length of time that passed after the blood test before my parents took me to Sick Children's Hospital in Toronto. The blood work showed raised creatine kinase (CK) levels that suggested there may be a problem in the muscles. CK is a muscle enzyme, which is released into the bloodstream at high levels when there is muscle fibre damage. The doctors ran a series of tests, including a muscle biopsy. In October 1975, at the young age of eleven, I was diagnosed with limb-girdle muscular dystrophy.

We didn't talk about our trip to Toronto; however, I do remember how I felt when I entered the hospital room. As the doctor left the room, my mom and dad had tears in their eyes. It was quiet in that hospital room—too quiet. I can't imagine how parents feel when their child has been diagnosed with a life-changing disease. Our family physician thought it best that my parents keep this information from me so it wouldn't upset or scare me. This seems pretty archaic by today's standards, but my parents took the physician's advice and sheltered me from my diagnosis. Life continued as normal.

One day in the fall of 1976, when I was in seventh grade and twelve years old, I came home from school upset. Some of the kids in class were talking about my disability. The gym teacher who taught grade seven took it upon herself to talk to the class about me and commented to the class that I had been recently diagnosed with muscular dystrophy. My friends knew what I had before I did. My mother was very upset and called the school principal. She was angry that my parents were not asked before the teacher spoke to the class. This became one of many occasions that people in my life informed me about my condition before my parents spoke to me.

My mother and I took the train for my yearly checkup to the Muscular Dystrophy Clinic at Sick Children's Hospital in Toronto. I can't remember a time when I wasn't anxious as the train approached Union Station in Toronto. I would tell my mother, "I am not staying in the hospital; I don't care what the doctors have to say!" This must have been so difficult for my mother to hear.

I remember when I started walking on my tippy toes. My calf muscles were so strong, overpowering the shin muscles, which caused the tendons around my ankles to tighten. It was virtually impossible to step on my heels. The doctors at Sick Children's Hospital suggested I have surgery to lengthen the tendons to relieve the pain I felt while trying to walk. This would also allow me to return to somewhat of a *normal* pattern of walking in which my heels could hit the ground before my toes. My parents consented to the operation. I did not have any aspirations of becoming a ballerina, so I agreed—not that I was given a choice.

I spent a week in the hospital. Two knee-high walking casts were put on my legs after the surgical technique of lengthening the Achilles tendon. I remember returning home from the hospital four days before Christmas 1977. I hated that hospital, but I do remember my grandma and grandpa visiting me. They bought me the cutest Raggedy Ann doll, which was later used in one of my watercolour paintings. Eight weeks after surgery, the casts were removed. I experienced a new sensation when my tiny heels hit the floor.

Prior to this procedure, the simple task of walking was painful. Compare a tendon to a rubber band that stretches to its full capacity. In my case, that rubber band or tendon expanded; however, it could not relax to its original size to allow elasticity or proper movement of my feet. The pain I once felt when walking had disappeared. Since the diagnosis of LGMD, this was the first time in my life when I wasn't ridiculed by other children. Non-disabled children can be cruel to young individuals who have physical limitations. I wanted to be able to walk similar to other children—free from embarrassment and humiliation. This surgical procedure is not often performed today. The doctors now feel it best to let children with this disease walk however need be without causing interruption and further weakness to the muscles during recuperation.

At a family gathering, I walked over to my mother and boldly asked, "Mom, am I going to die?" I only vaguely remember this and am not sure who was around. My mother must have been talking to her sisters and was shocked that I asked this question. I do know that my aunts and other family members cried as they spoke about this later. I know they felt for me and understood how terrified I must have been to come out and ask this scary question at the tender age of thirteen.

I remember hearing things like "I understand you will be in a wheelchair before you are twenty. You have that disease that the kids on the Jerry Lewis telethon have. Those kids die very young."

Limited edition print, Precious Treasures by Shelley Tudin

Talk about being scared to death. It wasn't until I was seventeen years old that I realized I didn't have one of the serious forms of muscular dystrophy; I wasn't going to die young.

For those of you who are not familiar with muscular dystrophy, the type I was diagnosed with is defined as:

> Limb-girdle muscular dystrophy (LGMD) Type 2 is a diverse group of disorders affecting the voluntary muscles, mainly around the pelvic (hip) and shoulder regions. Occasionally, the cardiac (heart) and respiratory (breathing) muscles may be involved. …The onset of LGMD may involve the pelvis, the shoulder area, or both. Early symptoms can include difficulty walking, running, and rising from the floor. Usually, and eventually, affected individuals will find it hard to climb stairs, stand up from a squatting position, and walk. Weak shoulder muscles can make it difficult to raise arms above the head, hold the arms outstretched, or carry heavy objects. The brain, the intellect, and the senses are not impaired. [1]

My two cousins Patty and Susan hosted a muscular dystrophy summer carnival in their backyard to help raise money for the Canadian Muscular Dystrophy Telethon, which aired on television every Labour Day. My uncle Gary made an appearance in his fireman uniform as he was our local

1   Muscular Dystrophy Canada, "Limb Girdle Muscular Dystrophy," www.muscle. ca/fileadmin/National/Muscular_Dystrophy/Disorders/430E_Limb_Girdle_MD_2007.pdf html (September 2007)

platoon chief in Brantford. I remember having fun at these carnivals but never realized my cousins were hosting these carnivals to help raise money for a disease that I had.

Those Awkward Teenage Years

Approximately four years later, when I was fifteen years old, my parents and I went to Sick Children's Hospital for my checkup. On this visit, the doctors questioned my parents about my sister and brother. They wanted to know if my siblings had any physical difficulties or changes. They suggested that the entire family come to the hospital for a series of blood work. Four months after this appointment, the entire family travelled to the hospital to have blood tests completed. Weeks later, my sister Michele, age sixteen, and my baby brother, John, age nine, were diagnosed with the same form of muscular dystrophy.

> Approximately 90 percent of LGMD is inherited as an autosomal recessive disorder. For someone to have one of these conditions, they have to have two faulty copies of the gene responsible. All of our genes come in pairs, one from our mother and one from our father. If someone has an autosomal recessive type of LGMD both of their parents must be carriers ….These parents will, together, have a 1 in 4 chance of having another baby with LGMD.[2]

---

2   *Ibid*

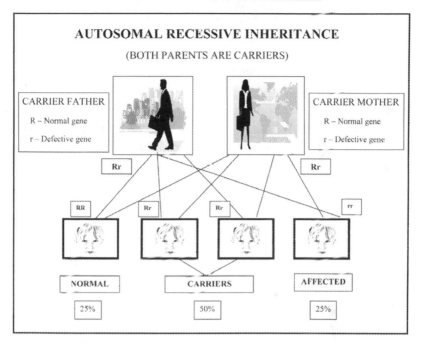

Genes are passed from both parents to a diagnosis of limb-girdle muscular dystrophy[3]

The geneticists explained that all three of my parents' children were passed a double dose of the same defective recessive gene. I believe the odds with all children affected are very slim (due to the 1 in 4 chance). We may be one of the only families in Canada where all the children have been affected with LGMD. No other immediate member of our family has been diagnosed with limb-girdle muscular dystrophy.

Exercise can help those with LGMD keep their muscles strong and limber. It is important, however, that they do not overexert themselves to the point of fatigue. During my middle teenage years, I joined a local swim club and swam three times a week. Swimming is the best exercise for those living with a neuromuscular disease. Swimming exercises all of the muscles. I also competed in the games for the physically disabled. I never won any of the swimming competitions, but it was a great experience meeting other disabled individuals from all over the world. I never felt different when I attended these competitions. For the first time in my teenage years, I felt accepted.

3   Retina Australia NSW Inc., "Autosomal Recessive Inheritance," www.google.ca/images from www.reinaaustraliansw.com.au (2008)

High school was tough for me. Trying to fit in with peers isn't easy as a young teenager. Having a physical disability made it even more difficult. Walking up and down stairs was becoming difficult for me to manoeuvre. The school I attended did not have an elevator until my senior year, so they allowed me to arrange my schedule so that all of my classes were upstairs during the first semester and downstairs during the second semester. I remember the embarrassment I felt as I struggled to get out of the school desk. Other students would stare at me as I experienced these difficulties.

I had to leave class early to get to my locker and my next class before the crowds of students entered the hallway. Many times, I didn't make my destination before students came storming out. Like a herd of elephants, the crowd of students knocked me over. Sometimes I got so frustrated. Being the gutsy person I was, I would say, "At least you could pick up my books since you never offered to help me up."

I wanted to have the full high school experience, including going to school dances and attending the prom. I was the cute girl in high school who was never invited to the prom. Every boy was afraid to ask the disabled girl out. Those who tried to ask me out were the biggest nerds. I may be disabled, but I had standards. Before you get the wrong idea, my definition of a nerd is a person who thought he was all that and more. These individuals had nothing intelligent to say and had no morals, goals, or career aspirations. Maybe I was too picky. I guess I should have been grateful that an able-bodied male wanted to be seen with me. Not on your life.

At sixteen, my older sister obtained her driver's license. Michele and I loved this new freedom to go places without our parents. My sister has always been physically stronger and less affected by LGMD than I. One Sunday afternoon, Michele drove my mother's car; we headed to visit our Grandma Kormos in West Brantford. Driving a little too fast, Michele turned a corner and my upper body toppled over, causing my head to fall into her lap. I started to laugh but quickly realized that I did not have the strength to sit up by myself, nor did my sister have the strength to push me off of her, especially while operating a vehicle. After arriving at our destination, Michele honked the car horn quite loudly so our grandmother would come outside and help me sit upright in the passenger seat. Once sitting, I was able to get out of the vehicle on my own. We thought it was funny that a sixty-year-old grandmother was stronger and in better shape than her fifteen-year-old granddaughter. Michele and I had a lot of fun on our ventures together.

Don't get me wrong, I enjoyed some good times during my high school years. I had several close friends. One of the highlights of my senior year was a trip to Paris, France. What a cultural experience! I thought Toronto, Ontario, Canada, was a large city. In 1982, Paris had a total geographical population of 3.4 million people, including the city and metropolitan areas. According to Toronto's latest census conducted in 2006, the city had 2.5 million occupants. Almost twenty-five years after I visited Paris, Toronto's population is still 1.5 million occupants shy of Paris's population when I visited in 1983.

At that time, Toronto had two main subway lines; Paris had more than twenty metro lines. Every evening, my fellow classmates and I were free to tour the city of lights as long as we were in a group. One evening, we decided to hop on the metro, to see the sights along the Champs-Élysées. The girls pushed me in an old rickety wheelchair that we rented for the week. I sat in the chair across from my friends on the metro. A mentally unstable man wandered over to me. I was a little leery as we all watched to see his next move. The man pulled down his drawers and proceeded to urinate on my feet.

There are disadvantages when you are disabled. Jumping out of a wheelchair quickly to avoid being urinated on is not one of them. Man, I really liked those pretty shoes that I had purchased earlier that day. What could I do, laugh or cry? My friends and I laughed so hard we almost wet our own pants. That incident wasn't the only mishap that night; we also got lost on the metro line. After a few panic attacks, and a very long ride, we safely arrived back at the hostel—tired and with soggy, smelly shoes.

Academically, I was a straight-A student. My goal was to attend college. I understood that the physical hardships were difficult, but my physical incapability did not define me as a person. I would put a smile on my face, slough it off, and march on (more like slowly walk) to my next class. I am sure my mother remembers me shedding a few tears, feeling like I did not fit in. In high school, being different was a curse. Little did I know then that those differences were a blessing in my life. I am a true testament that adversity builds character.

Off to University

fter completing high school in 1983, I decided to further my education at the University of Guelph. I excelled in art during high school, so it seemed fitting to focus my major area of study in fine arts with a business minor. It was exciting and scary moving away from home, not knowing what the future would hold. Moving to a new home and attending a new school is difficult enough, but adding a physical disability was a recipe for a nervous breakdown.

The first week at the university, also known as frosh week, was very entertaining. My bubbly personality was welcomed by the second-year students in my residence hall. I had a dozen new friends at the end of the first night after many good cheers at the local university pub. What my parents didn't know was their daughter was getting an education in Drinking 101.

Classes started as I motored on my new three-wheeled scooter to and from classes. This was the first time in my life that I had to use a motorized wheelchair. I hated that chair. It took more than a month before I would hold my head up high while driving. I'm surprised I didn't crash into any people or buildings. It wasn't until a young guy at a hall party came up to me and said, "You have such a pretty face, why do you look down all the time? You should be proud of who you are." This complete stranger changed my focus. He noticed my face, not just the wheelchair. I never looked down again while I rode my scooter. It allowed me to get to class without feeling exhausted.

I became accustomed to driving the scooter, but there was certain equipment that scooters offered that was definitely off limits: flags, bumper stickers, and carriages. These items were definitely not part of the cool accessories. I remember flying back and forth to classes with my books at the base of my scooter where my feet rested. One day, I wasn't aware that two very expensive books had fallen off. Having to buy two new books valued at more than one hundred dollars was not very cool.

The girls in my hall loved to place bumper stickers on the back of my scooter when I was occupied. They knew I loved those stickers, especially the ones that read, "Not so close—I hardly know you." Did they really think I needed any more attention? Didn't they know I wasn't like other wheelchair users? I was the cool chick in the scooter.

I remember feeling frightened when entering high school and trying to find the correct room. Direction was on a much larger scale at the university. Finding the correct building was the first step; finding a handicapped accessible entrance was the second. If I found my way into the building, I would look for an elevator to get to the floor where my class was held. As time passed, I became familiar with the campus layout. The once enormous mountain had become a molehill.

The first month of my first semester at Guelph was memorable. I felt like a young child at summer camp with this newfound freedom from my parents. The parties were endless. One evening, I decided to go into the hall lounge to do some reading. As I dove into the first chapter of Psychology 101, a loud roar occurred. It sounded like a herd of elephants coming down the hall. I saw hundreds of men running, and one was headed right for me. *Oh no,* I thought. *This is one of those panty raids they warned us about.* Someone screamed for us to shut the doors. The hall doors slammed shut, one after the other. It wasn't a panty raid, it was a female raid. Some big, strong, handsome fellow scooped me up, carried me down two flights of stairs, and put me on a large truck covered in bales of hay.

I still remember my roommate laughing out our bedroom window. "Have fun, Shelley," she yelled as two huge flatbed trucks pulled out of Macdonald Hall. Even though I was a little scared, I thought, *What the hell? Let's make the best of this situation.* It turned out that half of my floor was on the truck with me and half of us were not wearing any shoes. As we drove through the campus, we picked up more and more female victims. I still laugh about the girl they ambushed carrying her groceries home. She wasn't even a college student. They left her groceries all over the sidewalk. I couldn't help but think that these guys were a bunch of animals. It wasn't until later that I realized how these men came about this wild journey.

All of the first-year engineering students were sent letters to meet at a certain location for a pre-entrance exam. About two hundred anxious men arrived to write their exam. As they started to look over the exam, panic seemed to strike their faces. None of them had a clue how to answer the first few questions until they hit question six. It read, "This is not really an exam. We needed to get you all here." The senior engineering students who had written the letter started handing out lots and lots of beer. With the test anxiety suddenly removed from the first-year students, these young engineers seemed more relaxed. Subsequently, they explained what was about to happen. "As engineers, we have a reputation to uphold. We are having a corn roast off campus, and we need some persons of the opposite sex to join us. There are two huge flatbed trucks outside. The object of this game is to collect as many lovely females across campus to join us at this shindig." A loud "yahoo" followed.

We all had fun eating corn and drinking a few too many beverages. There was only one problem: How was I going to get back to the dorm? They couldn't have kidnapped me with my scooter; no, that would have been too easy. A few of us started to walk back. One brave soul decided to carry me piggyback. We seemed to be doing fine until a campus police officer stopped us. He said, "Can I see some ID, ladies?"

One girl spoke up with slurred words. "Well, officer, we don't have any ID; we were kidnapped by these crazy men." The officer was not sure how to respond.

Jill, the girl who was carrying me, also replied, "My friend is disabled, and we were wondering if you could give us a ride home." The officer never looked at our IDs; we never got a ride back to the dorm. I guess he never really believed that I was disabled. I don't think Jill ever piggybacked me after that.

During my first year of university, I was able to walk without the assistance of a cane or walker. I lived in Macdonald Hall, which was an all girls' residence. Fortunately, I could get in and out of bed on my own. Our dorm had many single, double, and triple rooms. Each floor had two large washrooms with a couple of showers in each. I could get on and off the toilet by pushing on my legs to get into the upright position. The only physical difficulty I had was getting up from the floor when I lost my balance and fell. Finding me on the ground after a fall became a weekly occurrence. My hall mates never hesitated in assisting me up. The first fall was embarrassing, but after time, everyone came to my rescue and lifted me back into a standing position.

There were so many "it could only happen to me" incidents during my time at the university. I remember one evening during first year, my roommate and I ventured out to our psychology class. It was a three-hour lecture; however, I don't ever recall staying longer than an hour and a half. Paula and I used to leave at break and stop at Derk Keller's, a local cafeteria/evening pub on campus. That evening, I was not using my scooter because it had a flat tire. After walking back to our dorm, Paula and I got the giggles. When you're disabled, it's very hard to walk and laugh at the same time. Hence, I fell on my butt. Paula tried to lift me up, but she was so weak from laughing that she was dying to use the facilities. "I'll be right back," she stated. "Otherwise, I'm going to wet my pants."

As I patiently sat in our first floor hall dorm waiting for Paula to return, another girlfriend passed by and saw me on the ground. We decided to have a little fun with Paula. Before she returned, my friend picked me up and left me standing near the wall. She then ran and hid around the corner so Paula could not see her. The look of astonishment on Paula's face was priceless. She asked, "Shelley, how did you get up?"

Keeping a straight face, I replied, "I crawled over to the wall, slowing walking my hands up my legs until I could grab the wall to stand upright."

Amazed, she asked, "Really? You got up by yourself?"

"Yes, I really did it myself."

Once again she asked, "Really?"

Once again I answered, "Really." A few seconds passed as I watched in horror as Paula approached me. Using both hands, she pushed me right over; back on my butt I went. "Now let me see you get up," Paula said.

A mutual friend came running around the corner. "Oh, Shelley, I can't believe she just did that!" Well, if I wasn't sore after the first fall, I certainly was after the second. I guess I deserved that one.

Homecoming at Guelph was always an eventful weekend. During my second year of college, my cousin Sue decided to hang out with me for the homecoming weekend. After pub hopping, we joined the campus street dance outside of Johnson Hall, which was one of the all-male residences. We bumped into a few of Sue's old high school friends from Brantford who resided in Johnson Hall. We decided to head up stairs for a few beverages; however, there was one problem. I could not get the key out of my scooter. It was jammed in so tight, we couldn't pull it out. If we could get the key out, the power would not activate. The wheels would lock and no one would be able to drive my scooter. But being the trusty, naive one, I made the call to leave the scooter outside the dorm. We were only going to stay for thirty minutes.

Thirty minutes had a way of turning into four hours. After a few beverages, Sue and I fell asleep in the guy's dorm room. At 5:00 a.m., we wandered out of Johnson Hall with wild, messy hair and smelling like a brewery. There was no scooter. I panicked. "My scooter is gone." As we tried to collect our thoughts, a few morning stragglers said they thought they had seen two guys going for a joy ride down a flight of stairs on a scooter.

We decided to head to the campus police. As we knocked on the door, a university officer came out to greet us. Let me tell you, we were not a pretty sight. The good news was that they rescued my scooter from the joy riders. I was so thankful but extremely embarrassed as they lectured me about leaving my wheelchair unattended.

I spent four years at the University of Guelph. I can honestly say this experience changed me as a person. I didn't know that I could overcome so many obstacles. Driving my scooter on campus in the winter was a tad difficult and extremely frustrating. Snow removal—or should I say lack of snow removal—made my blood boil. If I had a dollar for every time a person said, "You should put chains on those tires," I could have made a fortune and quit school. Perhaps these students thought chains on my tires would give my scooter better traction while travelling through deeper snow or stop the scooter from sliding on ice patches. Had the snow removal people majored in common sense, I probably would not have been stuck so many times.

At times, my scooter was used by other students as a source of winter entertainment. At times, a few brave people grabbed onto the back of my scooter as I went down the rather large ramp near the campus library. Who was I to say no to their winter daredevilish pranks? Even driving in fair weather could be trying. The campus walkways were often crowded. One afternoon, I was crossing College Avenue when the green light quickly turned to amber. I rushed across the road aiming for the cut-out ramp on the sidewalk. A large group of disrespectful students were in no hurry to move aside so I could use the ramp. As I turned to my left, I was staring at a car heading right for me. At that moment, I made a quick decision—hit the curb or be hit. You guessed it: I hit the curb and over I went, banging my head as I let out a loud profanity. (Had I not made that decision, only God knows how I would have ended up—severely disabled or possibly dismantled with body parts all over College Avenue!) The professor of the class that I was heading to was right behind me. Thankfully, he helped me and put the scooter upright. My professor walked beside me as I drove my bruised body and ego to class.

During my last year of college, I suffered from clinical depression. The endless hours of reading, doing assignments, writing essays, and taking finals takes a toll on young students. Trying to balance academic studies, a social life, proper nutrition, and sleep (or lack of sleep) can creep up and pack a wallop. The anxiety I was feeling was frightening. I was mentally and physically exhausted. Clinical depression is so debilitating. I felt as though I was trapped in a very deep hole that was impossible to climb out of. With a lot of support from my family, my physician, and my counsellor, I managed to dig myself out of this depression one day at a time. Anxiety and depression can be so frightening. Without this experience, I would not have gained personal empowerment and developed a greater inner strength and conviction to focus on the good things in my life. My doctor and my counsellor explained to me that it took a long time of self-destructive behaviour and negative thinking to become clinically depressed. There is no quick fix when it comes to overcoming depression.

During the summers, I worked to help pay my way through university. In February 1988, I was in my final months of school. Soon, I would no longer be able to hide in this social bubble. I applied to teachers' college but was not accepted that year.

Primary school seemed to have the highest applications in my graduating year, which may explain why I was not accepted.

It turns out that Baby Boomers aren't as eager to retire as expected. And many of those who do snap up coveted part-time substitute teacher positions to pad their wallets. In fact, between the Ontario and American programs boosted in the early '90s to help alleviate Ontario's looming teacher shortage are producing more than seven thousand more teachers than are retiring each year.[4]

Applying for teachers' college was an option, but it was not the most important priority in my life at that time. After four years of academia, I needed a break from school.

---

4   Considering teachers' college in Ontario? Think again. New report shows an excess of teaching graduates. www.macleans.ca/education/universities/article.jsp?content. Erin Millar & Marco Ursi. November 26, 2007.

On a sunny afternoon in June 1988, I graduated from the University of Guelph with a major in fine arts and a minor in consumer studies/business. My parents, my cousin Sue, and my dear uncle Ken, an alumnus of Guelph, cheered as I drove onto Johnson Field to receive my degree. Wow, I'd finally done it! All those challenges—the physical, the mental, and the academic ones—had all been worth it.

Shelley's University of Guelph Graduation, 1988

Since my graduation from the university, various policies and procedures have been established throughout Canadian educational facilities to assist students with physical, mental, and learning disabilities. Accessible learning departments assist students overcoming physical barriers, such as building accessibility, easy access through doors, seating arrangements, wheelchair ramps, disabled parking, and the like. No such organization existed when I attended the University of Guelph.

Today, accessible learning centres assist students with attention deficit hyperactivity disorder or acquired brain injuries or learning, hearing, vision, medical, physical, or psychological/emotional disabilities. Services may include note-taking, extra time for exam writing, adaptive computer devices, alternate format materials for textbooks, and organizational support for learning disabilities.

A New Life

A new chapter in my life was about to begin. I was now a potential money earner. I saw myself working for a marketing company in an art department. The last thing I thought I would do was freelance art work. I knew I was a talented artist, but there were so many other struggling artists out there who were just as skilful. After completing university at the age of twenty-two, I moved back to my family home in Brantford, Ontario. I found it difficult to live with my parents again after being on my own for four years. At the time, I received a monthly disability allowance called ODSP (Ontario Disability Support Program). Disabled individuals who are eligible can collect this income when they turn eighteen. I continued to work on various art pieces while I searched for office employment. I created commissioned paintings and drawings for local clients.

About a year later, I met my future husband. We travelled to various art shows to exhibit my paintings around Southern Ontario. My mother and sister attended some shows to help with the setup. I was pleased to have many envious fans of my work. Many people entered my booth, asking who the artist was. They were shocked when they found out the artist was in a wheelchair. At first, it bothered me to think that people assumed a disabled individual could not produce wonderful art. As time passed, I used my disability as an advantage. There were so many artists out there—how many of those talented artists were disabled with muscular dystrophy? Hopefully, they would remember my differences and my artwork.

I volunteered on the paediatric floor at our local hospital. Young children who are hospitalized because of illness are understandably frightened. I was familiar with this fear and anxiety. Any time I could spend with children in the hospital, whether to teach art and crafts or offer emotional support was important to me. Around the Christmas season, I spent extra time on the children's ward painting windows for the festive season.

Original watercolour el pasaje by Shelley Tudin

Original watercolour Le Cafe a Paris by Shelley Tudin

Original watercolour A Summers Afternoon by Shelley Tudin

I remember the first few weeks when I started dating the man who I later married. I wasn't sure if he was the one, but as time went by, he seemed to accept me—disability and all. Once a group of guys approached him at a local bar and yelled, "Hey, David, what's a cute girl like that doing with you? Does she feel sorry for you? Are you one of Jerry's Kids?"

He replied, "I'm not one of Jerry's Kids, but she is." These men didn't know how to respond to that remark.

There were many occasions when people said hurtful remarks about my unusual walk. "Walk much?" or "Are you drunk?" were questions I remember hearing all too often. Although these comments hurt me, I knew they were said out of ignorance.

Each year, over Labour Day weekend, the Muscular Dystrophy Association in the United States and Canada holds a telethon to raise money to assist children and adults with muscular dystrophy. The term "Jerry's Kids" refers to actor and comedian Jerry Lewis, who hosted the telethon from its 1966 inception until 2010, and those who have muscular dystrophy. The telethon is televised yearly and is now hosted by a different celebrity. In 1992, I painted the official Canadian Muscular Dystrophy Christmas card that was distributed around the country to raise money for MD and was recognized for this achievement on the Labour Day telethon televised in Toronto.

Physically speaking, my condition had not changed or progressed over the previous five years. My parents, my siblings, and I continued with our annual neurologist appointments at London Health Sciences. The geneticists suggested that my parents, my siblings, and I undergo more blood tests to confirm that the diagnosis of limb-girdle muscular dystrophy was indeed correct. The blood results confirmed the same diagnosis as the other tests had fifteen years earlier. The most astonishing news about my blood work was the knowledge that there was no further destruction of the muscles. The doctors could not explain this remission, but no one was more pleased than I.

My boyfriend and I continued to build our relationship. We dated for five years before he asked me to marry him. I felt so happy. I never thought I would have the opportunity to find love. In my mind, I believed that love, happiness, and marriage were for able-bodied people. It takes a strong, secure individual to understand and support a person with a physical disability.

On September 21, 1996, after five years of cohabitation, a total of six years together, we were married. This was one of the happiest days of my life. I remember my mother and father that day. My father said to my mom, "She looks so beautiful, doesn't she?" I knew my father was so proud to see one of his daughters getting married. Our wedding was quite large. We had seventeen people in our wedding party with more than three hundred guests invited to the reception. I remember being so nervous that day as were my parents—my sister, Michele, and I had inherited our parents' nervous stomachs. All four of us had to take some Imodium so we didn't have any unfortunate accidents during the ceremony.

The minister who married us specifically asked the bridal party to be at the church early—at least thirty minutes prior to the ceremony. I remember him asking me if we should have rented the Toronto Sky Dome for the large event. After visiting the salon for hair and makeup, the girls and I returned to my parents' home to get dressed for the big day. None of the bridesmaids were ready when the photographer arrived. The house was extremely chaotic as we hurried to get ready for the big day. Once the photographer snapped enough pictures at my parents' house, he headed over to the church.

The girls in the wedding party, including me, started to panic when the limo had not arrived twenty minutes prior to the wedding ceremony. One of the neighbours was pulling out of their driveway and heading for the church, so we asked them if some of the girls could catch a ride.

My sister and I got into our parents' car. It was apparent that the limo and driver was a no-show. At ten minutes to three, just as we were pulling out of the driveway, the limo arrived. The driver apologized and explained that his vehicle had had a flat tire on the way to my parents' place. Quite boldly, my friend Lori told the limo driver to leave, that he was not needed. I yelled from my parents' car, "No don't leave, I will still need you to take us and the champagne from the church to the park for pictures." I was probably the only bride in history who did not get to ride in the limo to her own wedding. At least the remaining attendants enjoyed the limousine ride to the church.

On the way to the church, my mother was driving, and I sat in the front seat next to her. My father and sister Michele sat in the backseat. Seemingly from out of nowhere, a young boy ran in front of the car. My mother quickly reacted and slammed on the brakes. What else could go wrong! Wearing a beautiful princess wedding gown and a tiara on my head, I yelled out, "Get the *bleep* off the road! We have a wedding to get to!" I still remember my father laughing hysterically as his angelic-looking daughter blurted out those not-so-angelic words. Once we arrived at the church, there was no time to be nervous. My father was still laughing as we were about to walk down the aisle.

Shelley and flower girl Samantha, September 21, 1996

Married life passed by as I continued to paint. But unfortunately, my freelance commissions did not bring in as much money as I would have liked. I continued my part-time work at a local bridal salon and later at a local bank. My husband wanted me to work full time. I became frustrated that the twenty-eight to thirty hours I worked outside the home plus the three to six hours I spent teaching watercolour classes, along with painting the odd commission, was not enough for him. One day, he made me so mad that I yelled out, "I shouldn't have to work." In retrospect, I should not have said that. I wanted the nice home and trips as much as he did.

We owned a beautiful home and an amazing dog. Ebony was an eighteen-pound cockapoo (part poodle and part cocker spaniel). Our little dog, who loved to play with socks, was trained to bring me the cordless phone. We started to train him by slipping the phone inside a sock. After a couple of weeks and a lot of cheese rewards, he learned the phone and the sock were one in the same item. The sock—which he used to carry the phone—was cut smaller and smaller until only a small piece of sock hung on the clip. We further trained him by hiding the phone anywhere in our house and then say, "Ebony, bring Mommy the phone." He searched every room in the house until he found the phone and brought it to me. The real test was asking Ebony to retrieve the phone when I was in an emergency situation.

One morning while getting ready for work, I could not get up from the raised toilet seat. *Ebony,* I thought, *you've got to come through for* me. "Ebony, go get Mommy the phone," I yelled. He immediately came into the bathroom; I repeated the demand once again. He started searching for the phone. I couldn't believe what a smart dog he was. He brought me the phone and dropped it on the floor beside me. I begged him to hand me the phone, but he didn't understand. Mommy didn't have any cheese for him. Unfortunately, I could not reach the floor to grab the phone to call for help. I started to panic. My wheelchair transit driver would be arriving any minute. All I needed was one of my male drivers to knock on the door while I was sitting on the raised toilet seat with my drawers hanging around my knees. I hoped the driver would be female.

I heard a knock at the door as a male voice yelled, "Shelley, are you okay?" I embarrassedly explained to him that I was indisposed and kindly asked him to call my mother. He radioed the office to send another bus within thirty minutes so I could get to work. Ten minutes later, my mother arrived to assist me in the bathroom so I could be ready for the next driver. I always thought that I would be on the ground from a fall when Ebony would come to my rescue. Some things never work out as you expect.

We talked about having children before we married and decided it would be too risky for my health. I wanted my husband to be sure that he would not regret later in life that he chose to be with me. He told me that my disability had nothing to do with him not wanting children. I respected his decision. However, if he had said, "Shelley, let's have a child," I would have tried. I remember a day when we were at my in-laws' house. Somehow, the conversation turned to the topic of having children. My husband may have been talking about having a vasectomy to his mom. She was adamantly opposed to this and thought I should be the one to have a tubal ligation even though she knew it would be difficult for me to go under anaesthesia.

I always felt his mother cared about me but wished her son would have married a healthy woman—one who could have given her son children. She said, "It would be very selfish of you to have a child." That comment deeply hurt me. I guess she thought a disabled woman would not be able to do all the necessary tasks of raising a child. I knew it would be difficult to handle all the physical demands a child puts on a parent, but there is also emotional support and love. So many children with two physically healthy parents do not get the love and nurturing they deserve. She had no right to make that comment. The decision to have children was up to my husband and me. I would never have a child unless he was a willing partner. I was well aware that I would have needed a lot of assistance. Had the situation been different, I would have loved to become a mother.

Living with a neuromuscular disease does not necessarily mean never having children of your own. However, it is important to discuss with your neurologist the risks of giving birth to a child born with muscular dystrophy. I have an autosomal recessive disease, which means two defective genes are inherited from both parents. In my case, my partner would have to carry the same mutated gene in order for our child to have muscular dystrophy.

Along with the genetic component, the health risks that could occur during pregnancy and childbirth should be discussed with a doctor. Most women with muscular dystrophy do not have the muscle strength to push a child through the birth canal. A caesarean section would be performed to ensure a safe delivery for mother and child.

The last component requires the ability to lift and take care of your child. Although this would be difficult, there are support options for child care. Family and friends may be willing to offer a helping hand. If finances allow, disabled parents can hire a private nanny service to assist with their children. A personal support worker is provided free of charge, by the Canadian government, to assist the disabled person or parent with the tasks of daily living. For those who reside in the province of Ontario, fourteen Community Care Access Centres provide in-home community-based health care services for you or for a loved one.[i]

During the late-nineties, I was walking with a cane. I could safely get in and out of bed and the shower on my own. There were times I would fall, but luckily, I had not suffered any serious injuries other than a few cuts and bruises. If I needed help when my husband was at work, I called the closest friend or family member to come over and help me back on my feet. This was a weekly occurrence, but I continued to walk around the house and use the scooter for outside trips. Since my teenage years, the limb-girdle muscular dystrophy had not done any further damage to my muscles. Unfortunately, my personal life as a married woman was not so stable. My husband and I experienced many power struggles regarding our finances and our lack of quality time together.

In all fairness, my ex and I both contributed to the difficulties in our marriage. We argued a lot. As a young girl, I remember my parents arguing about my father's heavy alcohol consumption. My husband suggested I attend counseling to deal with some of the unsuccessful coping strategies that I'd developed as a young child. When our lives were peaceful and happy, I would start an argument about something that may have bothered me weeks earlier. I began attending weekly Al-Anon meetings. I discovered that children who were raised in a household with a problem drinker suffered from low self-esteem and the insecurities that accompanied these feelings of defeat and loss of control. Alcoholism is a family disease that affects all members in the household. By attending weekly meetings and going to individual counseling, I discovered I was a loving person. The difficulties of my childhood did not define me as a person. The counsellor explained that I subconsciously recreated that drama of conflict during my marriage as I had once experienced it as a child. With this newly acquired knowledge from counseling, I learned to deal with conflict and to respect others. Most importantly, I learned to believe in myself. When a conflict between my husband and I escalated, name calling and all, I tried to use my new skill and state, "Please do not talk to me like that. I am a person, and I deserve respect."

He often replied, "What happened to that sweet girl I fell in love with?" Sometimes my temper got the better of me and I slipped into my old patterns. I truly think this new confidence made him feel uncomfortable. I loved my husband dearly, but I felt as though I was the only one trying to work on our relationship. Despite these issues, our married life continued on.

I have always had a big heart and am willing to lend a helpful hand to someone in need. One morning, two weeks before Christmas, the wheelchair transit driver arrived at our home to drive me to work. When he mentioned a client who had no finances to purchase a winter coat, I turned back into my house and asked the driver to grab a winter coat that I no longer wore. I asked him to offer my coat to the woman so she could stay warm for the winter. A week later, the same driver said this woman was so grateful and had cried tears of happiness. Countless people are less fortunate, and any random act of kindness is the greatest gift we can offer.

In 1997, my brother John moved in with my husband and me. At this time, John was single and working full time as a graphic artist. Physically speaking, my brother used a cane to walk around the house. Unlike me, he had obtained his driver's license at age sixteen and was still able to drive his vehicle without any difficulties.

It was nice having my brother live with us. John has always had a lot of friends, so plenty of people dropped in for visits. My husband, my brother John, and I were big hockey fans, and I am ashamed to admit we were all die-hard Toronto Maple Leaf fans.

One afternoon, my brother and I arrived home from work around the same time. He had made his way down to his bedroom when I heard a loud bang. John immediately started screaming, "Help! Shelley, please find some help." His yelling intensified. I tried to drive my scooter down to his room. John had fallen and his leg was wedged between the wall and his water bed. He yelled out, "My leg is going to break!"

I reached my husband by phone, but he knew he would not be able to get home quickly enough to assist. By this time, I was shaking. I felt completely helpless that I couldn't provide any assistance to my brother. While I was on my scooter, I managed to open the door, drive down the ramp, and drive erratically across the street to a neighbour's house. My dog Ebony had followed. Not able to drive up the step to their front door, I loudly yelled, "Help!"

By the time my friend ran to my house, the young girl who lived next door came running over as well. They both ran into the house to aid John. Most of the neighbours must have heard my brother yelling. I was a nervous wreck and so frightened for him that I could not enter the house. I put my head down on my scooter and cried as I said a prayer for him. "God, please let my brother be okay. He has already broken one leg. He cannot go through the pain of another broken bone and surgery." The women came out of the house five minutes later. They explained that he was sore but his leg was in one piece. I was so thankful. I went inside the house to talk to John, who commented on how grateful he was that I had reacted so quickly. It is amazing how adrenaline takes over in an intense situation and allows your body to accomplish tasks you might otherwise not be able to do.

A Trip to the Dominican Republic

Despite the hard times, we had a great, loving family and a lot of wonderful friends. In addition to visiting Mexico, we were fortunate to travel to many of the Caribbean Islands, including Barbados, St. Lucia, the Dominican Republic, and the Florida Keys in the American Caribbean. The most memorable incidences occurred while we visited the Dominican Republic.

In February 1997, we travelled to the Dominican Republic with our friends Mike and Marie and her family. The four of us had dinner reservations one evening. I had hopped into the shower, dried off, and slipped into a sundress. I was running behind schedule and still had to do my hair and makeup. Normally, I walked with my cane, but I thought I could save time by carrying my makeup bag in one hand and the hair dryer in the other as I manoeuvred toward the bathroom. Big, big mistake! Imagine falling backward and your head striking the terra-cotta floor before the rest of your body hits. I couldn't move or talk, but I could see my husband looking down at me. "I'm dying," I tried to say—but no sound came out. My ears were ringing. All I could hear was a high-pitched sound.

A short time passed before Mike and Marie arrived at our door. I started to cry. The resort doctor called an ambulance, which, in the Dominican, was a rickety old white van. Although the stretcher resembled our medical stretchers, it was only approximately five inches above the ground. What a bizarre ride to the hospital. The doctor arrived in a tank top and cut-off jean shorts. He X-rayed my skull and announced the diagnosis: a concussion.

I spent one night in a Dominican hospital. I was taken to a private room when the hospital found out I had excellent health insurance. Considering the blow I'd had to my cranium, I didn't feel too bad. My husband and I woke at 5:00 a.m. to the greeting of a rooster cock-a-doodling. I couldn't help but wonder if this was a figment of my imagination or if I was part of a cheesy 1970s movie. No, I wasn't delirious or dreaming. A rooster was outside my window; this was my morning wake-up call, except I wasn't at the resort.

I wanted out of that hospital, even though it had just been one night, and get back to the sun, my lawn chair, and a cold beverage. Later that week, we booked a Jeep safari. We ventured by Jeep over the countryside where the movie *Jurassic Park* was filmed. Part of the safari included a waterfall adventure. This was one adventure I would definitely not participate in. As the others headed to the waterfalls, our tour guide, Julio, who resembled a young Mohammad Ali, stayed back in the Jeep with me. Of course, I wanted to see those waterfalls.

Julio and I decided to make the best of it. We had a few beverages of Caribbean rum—151-proof Dominican rum. Wow, it was strong! An hour later, it suddenly hit me: I desperately had to go to the bathroom. I didn't have a built-in catheter. "Julio, we have a problem." What was I going to do? Julio began to shout to two female tour guides to assist me. He carried me to a grassy area, and the tour guides he summoned to help followed behind.

Julio was a perfect gentleman. He held the towel while two Spanish women tried to hold me in a squatting position. "Go pee, go pee," they said over and over again. I thought to myself, *Shelley, this is no time to be gun shy*. It would have been so much easier to explain in English how to assist a disabled girl. I couldn't hold the pose any longer. The ground was a little gritty, but my bladder felt so much better. Julio carried me safely back to the Jeep.

I still remember watching my friend Marie coming up the hill when she spotted me. "Oh no, Shelley is smoking a cigarette." I only smoked when I was tipsy. I still remember Marie laughing hysterically at me. "You crazy girl!"

A Family Tragedy

The next few years were the most difficult. I truly wonder how I kept it together. My mother has always been the strongest, most selfless woman I know. I can't remember a time that she ever refused to help my sister, brother, or me. Our mother handled her children's disabilities in a remarkable way. Our father had more difficulty coping with our disease. Despite his nervous nature, he loved us dearly and did the best he could. He was such a funny, witty individual. He had his share of problems, but he was a gutsy, honest, and hardworking man. My father had a drinking problem. Instead of feeling anger toward him, I offered him encouragement and support.

During December 1997, my father was not feeling well. My mother blamed my father's ailments on his drinking. Shortly after Christmas Day, I remember my father's face being a pasty white colour. Our family doctor asked him to come in for a blood test. I guess they were going to collect a complete blood count to see if he had an infection or was bleeding internally. His blood count was dangerously low. They immediately booked him for a gastrointestinal endoscopy and a colonoscopy. In early January 1998, my father was diagnosed with colon cancer. The surgeon booked him for a colectomy, which was scheduled to take place two weeks later. Once my father was diagnosed with cancer, everything seemed to blur for our family.

About a week later, my mother awoke to my father screaming out in extreme pain. My mother, who had worked in the emergency department of our local hospital for the past forty years, was on autopilot and immediately yelled at my dad to get out of bed. My father could not move at all. She called for an ambulance. During the next twelve hours in the hospital, physicians took x-rays and watched my father's condition turn from poor to grave. Once his abdomen started to distend, the surgeon rushed him into the operating room.

I sat with my mother for five hours—both of us were shaking. My mother kept praying that my father would make it through surgery. *What the hell is happening to my father?* I wondered. This was the longest five hours of my life. My aunts and uncles came up to the hospital while we all waited for any news about my dad.

Around 1:00 a.m., the surgeon stepped into the waiting area. He said, "Well, he made it through surgery. The next seven days will be crucial. The cancerous tumour in the colon had broken away, perforating the intestine wall, attaching itself onto the spleen, and rupturing it." My father had lost half of his colon and his entire spleen. They flushed him out as dangerous toxins travelled through his body. The doctor had started him on some powerful antibiotics so peritonitis would not set in. All we could do now was wait to see if he pulled through over the next few days. He was recovering in the intensive care unit. I wanted to yell out loud but nothing would come out of my mouth.

I didn't want my mother to be alone; she slept at our house that evening. She woke early the next morning and immediately called intensive care and was told that my father was resting comfortably. When my mother first saw my father in the hospital bed, tubes were coming out of every crevice on his body. He tried to talk but was drifting in and out of sleep.

The next morning, he seemed more alert. The surgeon came to see my father sometime later that day. He explained to my father that he had performed a bowel resection—a colonectomy—to remove the parts of the small and large intestine affected by the cancerous tumour. A colostomy was performed. This is an opening in the colon (intestine) which is attached to a hole in your abdominal wall. The opening in your skin may be called a stoma or an ostomy. With a colostomy, stool (bowel movement) comes out of this opening and into a sealed bag.

Two days after surgery, my father was walking up and down the hallways. The doctor commented that it was a miracle that he had survived surgery. Peritonitis usually causes heart failure. I guess my dad had an extremely strong heart and an incredible will to live. He stayed in the hospital for ten days. He recovered well, and we saw a lot of changes in my father that spring. He quit drinking and smoking and started walking four miles a day. My father gained all his weight back and more. I can't remember ever seeing my dad with such a protruding belly.

Approximately six months after his surgery, my father was able to walk his eldest daughter, Michele, down the aisle. Michele and Jim were married on June 6, 1998. It was a beautiful wedding.

My mother continued her part-time work as a ward clerk in the emergency department at our local hospital. Although my father turned over a new leaf, he did slip up on the odd occasion. This usually happened when my mother was working on a Saturday 3:00 to 11:00 p.m. shift. My father would head out to a local pub that was about a twenty-minute walk from my parents' home. I was glad that he would not drive his car if he had been drinking alcoholic beverages. Feeling a little intoxicated, he decided to make his journey back to the house before my mother arrived home from work. As he stepped off the curb to cross the road, he was hit by a car. He was thrown on to the dash of the car, rolled off, and fell on the road.

The two young men driving could not have been more than twenty years of age. They stopped and got out of their car to see if my father was still breathing. The first thing out of my father's mouth was, "Have you boys been drinking? You better leave before the police arrive." These two young gentlemen had not been drinking, but they were frightened. An ambulance arrived and took my father to the hospital. Luckily, he suffered only a few scrapes and bruises. I think my father thought he was a cat with nine lives; he survived the first two years of cancer, including two surgeries and chemotherapy. We were furious that he put himself in grave danger.

My mother and father celebrated their fortieth wedding anniversary on June 18, 2000. In August of that same year, my father was cutting the grass and felt very dizzy and fatigued. He had his regular cancer checkup later that week. It was the worst news he could receive. Not only had the cancer returned, but it now invaded his liver.

When cancer perforates and travels into the blood stream, attaching itself to another organ, it is referred to as stage four cancer. I am so happy my father was not told he was in stage four cancer after the original diagnosis. He had found a new lease on life and was so happy to be alive. It is often said that when someone has a life-altering experience, life is appreciated so much more. I can truly attest to this.

On January 27, 2001, my father lost his battle with colon cancer. He fought hard as we tried to comfort him, but he was in excruciating pain. The smell was strong and intense. We all knew my father's body was shutting down. My brother-in-law, Jim, and my sister, Michele, spoke to my dad while he was in a coma: "Dad, you are in so much pain. It's okay to let go. Don't worry about Mom. We will take care of her." My mother had left the hospital room to get a coffee downstairs at Tim Horton's. One minute later, my mother entered the hospital room, and my father took his last breath.

Dad and Shelley, September 2000

The funeral was surreal. I could not understand why my mother had to endure so much hardship when she gave so much. So many friends and family members offered their condolences at the funeral, but I don't think I heard any of them. Over the next six months, I shed tears on and off, mourning the death of my father. It's difficult to say good-bye to a loved one. My grandfathers and two very young cousins had passed, but coping with this loss was the most difficult. After the funeral, I remember yelling out loud, "I want my dad back—I want him back right now!"

I never felt I had the emotional support I needed and deserved from my husband. I cried myself to sleep for more than six months. My little dog Ebony licked every one of my tears. I can't remember many hugs from my husband during this difficult time in my life. I remember one particular comment that still burns deep in my soul. "Don't you think it is time you get over your father's death?" This comment, coming from a man who had never lost a parent, cousin, or close friend, was simply unforgivable.

A few months later, my husband's father was rushed into an operating room with a ruptured appendix. I offered my support, but he insisted I stay home. He comforted his mother while they waited for my father-in-law to come out of surgery. When my husband arrived home late that evening, I told him that everything would be fine. Even though peritonitis had set in, I explained that the antibiotics would fix him in no time. He discounted my comments as he said; "My father almost died tonight. You don't know how I feel."

I calmly replied, "No, I don't understand how you feel, my father died. Your father will make it through this." Apparently, my husband was the only person in the world who had experienced a scare with a father's health.

By 2002, it was apparent to me that I could not emotionally connect with my husband. I felt lost, even though I loved him dearly. He was charming and cordial in public, but at home he seemed indifferent. He spent most of his time on the computer. I cooked most of the meals, which he took downstairs to eat. I might as well have lived alone with Ebony. God knows he was more loving and supportive at that time in my life than the man I'd married.

I complained and complained and complained. It was like talking to a brick wall. I knew he was not happy and asked him about going to counseling, but he didn't seem too interested. We had a beautiful house, new cars, many Caribbean trips, a beautiful dog, and lots of family members and friends who loved us dearly. We did have many good times, but I knew something was going to happen to our marriage if we didn't try to deal with our conflicts. Was he having feelings of regret? Was marriage to a disabled person too much for him to handle? I tried to talk to him about how he was feeling and asked him several times if he still loved me.

The Accident

The following year, my husband and I decided to renovate our kitchen to make the room more accessible for me. I wanted to have easy access to the cabinets, the refrigerator, and stove with counters close by so that I could drag heavy objects without injuring myself. I enjoyed cooking and wanted to remain as independent as possible.

On September 8, 2003, my husband and I were completing our two-month renovation on our house when I experienced a terrible fall. I was in a lot of pain and do not remember much except yelling to my husband to get me a bucket and then vomiting into our crock pot. I immediately went into shock when I started rocking my head. My husband tried to comfort me and to move me into a more comfortable position. I remember cursing at him because the pain was so intense. The ambulance arrived within two minutes. What we didn't know at the time was that I had a spiral fracture on my left femur, which is the largest bone in the body and along which the femoral artery runs. If this artery severs, one could die within minutes.

Once again, my mother hurried to the emergency department. The medical staff rushed me to the imaging department to x-ray my left leg. When they explained to me that I had fractured my femur, my mother started to sob. I felt so bad that she had to see me in such pain. We both knew that fractured leg bones were the main reason why people with muscular dystrophy lose their ability to walk. I was quite agitated and insisted that I go home as I had to work in the morning. What was I thinking? Perhaps it had something to do with the morphine dripping into my veins.

I was scheduled for surgery the next evening. Understandably, I was very nervous. Those with muscular dystrophy do not do well under anaesthesia. The muscles around their lungs take longer to respond. Jim, my brother-in-law, came to see me an hour before the surgery. I felt touched that he visited the chapel and said a prayer for me. Thirty minutes prior to surgery, I fought with the surgeon to have this procedure done while under a local spinal anaesthesia. Eleven medical staff members waited for me to make a final decision regarding the best option for the surgery. My final decision was quickly made when the orthopaedic surgeon said, "Shelley, you strike me as a nervous person. I do not think you will be able to handle the sound of the saw cutting through your leg."

Terrified, I looked right at her and said, "What saw?" Not waiting for an answer, I quickly added, "Put me out, completely out." The medical staff, my mother, and my husband laughed and clapped after I made this important decision. They wheeled the stretcher that I was on into the operating room. During the five-hour surgery, a fourteen-inch titanium rod was inserted through my left femur. The rod was anchored by long pins, three above the knee and three at the thigh.

The following day, I couldn't believe that I was in the hospital and had survived a five-hour surgery. Once again, life threw a curve ball when I least expected it. My husband had to work that day, so I was grateful my mother and sister were at my bedside. I was happy to be alive. I remember my sister commenting to me, "Shelley, you look great." Michele is my best friend. We have always been there for each other. She even painted my toenails with colourful nail polish that day.

While I was in the hospital for six weeks, I missed my dog Ebony and my husband. I could hardly wait to go home to my boys and our new kitchen. I endured five weeks of painful rehabilitation and intense daily therapy. I remember how the needles that were inserted into my stomach stung. The Coumadin shots were necessary to prevent blood clots forming in my legs. The doctors thought I would never walk again. Little did they know how stubborn I was.

Approximately ten days after surgery, I stood up on my broken leg. I detested those long, white, tight stockings under the Zimmer splint. Two weeks into my stay, depression set in. I could not imagine where my life would take me from here. I said many prayers to my father and God: *Please give me strength to get through this rough patch in my life. I will never take anything for granted from this point on.*

I thank God for my dear mother, husband, sister, brother-in-law, brother, and the endless relatives and friends who visited me night after night on the rehab floor. With a lot of support and perseverance, I fought my way back on my feet, taking a few steps at a time.

Conflict and Depression—A Hostile Separation

I was released from the hospital in late October. I remember my husband saying, "I am so glad you are home. I really missed you." While I heard his words, I did not truly feel them. I sensed that he did not want me to return home. Female intuition told me something was terribly wrong. Two days prior to my Christmas Art Open House that I hosted every November, my husband told me that he no longer was in love with me. My world completely fell apart, or so I thought.

We tried counseling; however, I was the only partner willingly participating. I felt as though I was waiting for a bomb to go off. Christmas came and went. So did Valentine's Day. There were no cards or presents for me that season; however, money was available for my husband and partner of fourteen years to buy himself a new leather coat. I knew my husband could be selfish, but his true colours were clearly displayed as vibrant as one of my watercolour paintings. The pain from the injury to my left femur was intense. I remember asking my husband to massage my leg, but he would have no part of it. The anger and frustration I was feeling toward him was building.

It wasn't until the fighting became constant that I finally realized I had to leave. I remember saying to him, "You are so lucky that I cannot get up and kick the crap out of you. I could kill you for treating me like this. You make me feel worthless."

He went into our beautiful new kitchen and grabbed a butcher knife. He tried to force the knife into my hand. He yelled, "Kill me. Kill me if that is what you want." I knew it would be easy to snap, lose my mind, and finish him off. But I couldn't kill this man, a man I had loved for fourteen years who now felt like a stranger to me. At that moment, my life was over. I rationalized that he didn't deserve to live.

Thank God this disease called muscular dystrophy did not allow my tiny, thin arm to lift that butcher knife. I responded quite hastily, "You are not worth it!"

I cried and cried. I knew at that very moment, our fourteen-year relationship—thirteen years of cohabitation and eight years of marriage—were over. I phoned Michele and Jim. They told me to be strong and offered me a place to stay. I ordered an electronic bed and waited patiently for my purchase. I did not know how I would get through this separation. My heart told me to hold on to him, but my head told me our relationship was over. How much more could I endure?

One week later, I lost my dear, loving dog, Ebony. He had been with me for twelve years. He was the one sure thing that I was taking away from this marriage. Only one week had passed when my grandmother on my father's side, who had suffered a stroke the month before, took a turn for the worse and passed away. The following day, my ex lost his grandmother—five life-changing events in such a short time. How could one person handle all this sorrow? I have never felt so alone and scared.

A religious adage states that God gives you what you can handle. This is true and utter bullshit. I believe God gives more hardships to those who are the strongest. What I did not comprehend at the time was that someone was watching over me. He carried me when I could not walk and wiped my tears when they would not stop. What did I do that was so undeserving that I lost my husband? I thought I was a loving, caring wife. Despite my disability, I worked twenty-eight hours a week outside the home, taught painting classes in the evening, completed many commissioned watercolours, cooked dinner every evening, and did the laundry and cleaning. At thirty-nine years of age, I thought I looked cute and slim. I had a fun-loving personality and a strong determined nature to succeed. My father always told me that I was a great person, despite any physical differences, and deserved the best that life offered. If this was life, then I did not want any part of it.

I cried on and off for a year. Although living with my husband was difficult, I missed the person I fell in love with and my life with him as a married person. I spent half my living years with him. Once I heard the news that he had truly moved on, the anger set in. It was official. Three months after we separated, he was seen with someone else. What hurt the most was who he was seeing.

My husband and I had been quite close with a young woman I worked with and her fiancé. This couple was particularly special to me. They asked us to stand up for them at their July wedding. No wonder it hit me like a ton of bricks when I learned that my husband, from whom I was now separated, was dating the sister of my friend's fiancé. A few months earlier, I was asked to step out of my friend's wedding party. I immediately called my ex and asked him to do the same thing, even though it may have been a selfish act at the time. It was extremely difficult for me to be energetic and excited for two people that I thought were my friends. Anger makes a person do crazy things. A year later, I apologized to this friend for some of my actions; however, our relationship did not continue.

Many unanswered questions of why my marriage ended started to become clear. This young person of twenty-one years of age, thirteen years younger than my husband, had successfully caught his attention. Even though the difficulties in our marriage were evident, so many insecurities I felt over those past five months were clarified. Thinking back, I remembered that my husband and I attended a twenty-fifth wedding anniversary for my friend's parents in August 2003. I also remembered seeing my ex and this girl leaving the restaurant to have a smoke together.

I broke my leg in September 2003. He came to visit me every afternoon while I was in the hospital. In my opinion, I believe he spent his evenings on the Internet chatting to her, but I had no proof. By mid-October, it was clear that he wasn't the same person who had sat outside the hospital crying after he heard I had broken my leg and needed surgery. "Why her? It should have been me," he had said.

The crying finally stopped. Rage set in. I thought *that little witch. I invited her into my home and she flirted with my husband.* Looking back, it is funny how things happen. I was a trusting wife. I never imagined that my husband would end up with a woman half my age. My husband played hockey for a recreational league, and in February 2004, one month before we separated, this young woman grabbed my husband at the ice rink and introduced him to her parents. I thought it was rude that she did not introduce me as his wife, considering we were both in her brother's wedding party. We had not officially decided to separate at that time. When a married couple has relationship problems, it does not give a third person the right to interfere and try to break up that marriage. I am a strong believer in karma. If a man in a long-term relationship and marriage finds it so easy to walk away on his disabled wife, then it will be very easy for him to leave any woman he commits to—married or not and with or without children.

I truly believe he was cheating on me. He will deny it as long as he lives; the two of them are the only people who know the truth. I left my marriage with no guilt. I tried everything humanly possible to save our marriage, but both partners must be willing to make it work.

There were a couple of times when my anger got the better of me. During my first summer being separated, I would watch my brother-in-law play hockey since I was living with my sister and him. Most of our mutual friends that I had hung around with before the separation did not want to associate with me after the split. Most of my couple friends did not want to choose sides between my ex and me. Now I know the loneliness people felt years ago when they were diagnosed with an infectious disease and placed in quarantine.

A special couple, very close to me, from St. Catherine's, Ontario, continued to support me throughout this separation. Stephanie and I and our spouses met in 2002 on a trip to the Mayan Riviera in Mexico. One Sunday afternoon, in the summer of 2004, Stephanie drove me to Jim's hockey game. The young girl, who my husband was now dating, made an appearance at the hockey arena. When I saw her for the first time, my heart raced and sank. It felt as though my heart was about to explode from my chest. I never wanted to face or be in the presence of this young woman, fearing I would say something rude and regret it later. After the game finished, Stephanie pushed me in my manual wheelchair as we left through the back door on the ice level entrance. As we exited through the door, I spotted this person. Stephanie told me to keep quiet but my intense feelings of rage overpowered me and I blurted out, "Stephanie, do you smell that?" She looked at me with this deadly stare when I repeated the same words, "Stephanie, do you smell that?

Stephanie glared back at me when she realized she could no longer control my comments and asked, "Smell what?"

I blurted out, "You can't smell that, Stephanie? All I can smell is white trash!"

My ex's girlfriend looked at me but was speechless for a moment. When my dear friend and I approached her vehicle, we heard a loud backlash of nasty comments. She yelled, "Ah, is the poor disabled girl upset because her husband left her for me? Cry me a river."

I had tears in my eyes but never responded. My friend Stephanie, who I have never heard curse in the two years I had known her, shouted back, "You better shut your bleeping mouth before I come over there and shut it for you. Have you no compassion? Shelley is angry and hurt; she feels betrayed by both of you. How would you feel if some young girl half your age went after your husband after you had lived together fourteen years? You would be just as devastated."

She commented back, "Poor, disabled Shelley, cry me a river." We decided that speaking to this person was a waste of time. My comment toward her was not very nice, so, of course, she was only going to defend herself. What bothered me the most was she seemed to have no sympathy toward me and felt no guilt.

A few months later in the fall, still living with my sister and her husband, I travelled to the rink once again. This time, it was to watch my brother-in-law play hockey. I decided to drive my wheelchair past my ex's new girlfriend, whose brother also played hockey in the same league. I thought I heard her yell something nasty. My blood started to boil as my face turned three different shades of reddish purple. "Are you referring to me?" I asked. The table of people she sat with were silent.

I then heard a comment from her and her stepfather: "Whore." Wow, that was the first time I was ever referred to as a whore. I always thought I was the oldest living virgin at the age of twenty-three. This was not a word that represented a long-time married woman who was monogamous for more than fourteen years.

She then commented on how I was trying to take all of her boyfriend's money and continued by asking how I dared try to get alimony from him. We had been fighting among our lawyers and had not come to any sort of an agreement as to who got what after our separation. Our matrimonial home had sold, and our debts had been paid. At that time, I believe we had $70,000 dollars in a frozen joint bank account. Our assets, including furniture, appliances, artwork, and personal belongings may have totaled $30,000.

I calmly responded, "That money of your boyfriend's is half mine. If you were so worried about your boyfriend paying alimony, maybe you should have thought about this before you started sleeping with a married man!" The next thing I saw was this young woman coming at me with a swinging arm and clenched fist. A gentleman on my brother-in-law's hockey team stopped her. More harsh words were exchanged before I left in tears. Anyone who throws a punch at a disabled person does not belong in the same class as my friends and family.

I knew that the two of them deserved each other. I could do so much better. It may have taken two years of self-talk and counseling for me to truly believe this, but one day it happened. I was lonely but realized that I was worthy of true, selfless love. I prayed every night to God and my father that I would experience real love again. I wanted the anger and pain to stop. A few men asked me out for dinner, but nothing special developed.

On July 22, 2004, five months after our separation, my family and I celebrated my fortieth birthday. The party was held at my mother's house on Kensington Avenue. Seventy-five relatives and friends enjoyed a barbeque, swimming, beverages, cake, ice cream, and a lot of good times. When a person experiences a life-changing event, the importance of family is recognized. A spouse may come and go, but it's those people who are most dear to you that stand by and hold you up during the hard times. My family's support made me strong.

Standing Alone, Standing Strong

Feeling very discouraged, as though I just existed in life and was not actually living it, I decided to see a spiritualist. I wanted someone to tell me that my life did have meaning and things were going to get better. The spiritualist spoke to me for an hour. Her words offered some wisdom and encouragement. She did see a future husband in my life. She also spoke of a father figure and a little black dog that had passed.

One comment surprised me. She told me that my ex left me because he wanted to have a family of his own. That hurt—I would have loved to be a mother. The spiritualist was correct. Years later, my former husband had two children with his new girlfriend.

The spiritualist also mentioned a medical problem but told me not to worry about it. My doctor would discover it during a routine exam. These cells would be removed before any damage could spread and cause me harm. The last thing we talked about was my financial situation. When she repeatedly mentioned how financially successful I would become, I asked, "Am I going to win the lottery?" She explained that the rewards would come from something that I was going to create. I don't know if I believed everything she said to me, but I left there with a glimpse of hope for my future.

I am so thankful that my sister, Michele, and her husband, Jim, opened their hearts and their home to offer me the support and love I so desperately needed. I worked full time at a call center. It was not the best job. But at least I was getting up out of bed with the help of my home care workers and trying to put the pieces of my life back together. Since the break to my left femur, I could no longer get out of bed on my own. I continued to meet with my family law lawyer, hoping to come to some agreement with my ex-husband. Unlike my legal fees, a large portion of my ex's legal fees were covered by his employer's union. I was not going to give in. The amount of alimony I was asking for was a small amount in relation to his monthly net income.

My lawyer assured me that things would work out regardless how long this matter went on. Many times, I left his office crying but continued to fight and remain strong. We finally attended a court conference along with our lawyers to come to some kind of agreement. My ex-husband did not feel I deserved one cent of alimony. The judge explained to him that the amount of alimony I wanted was very reasonable. Still, he did not want to agree to that amount until my lawyer backed him into a corner.

The judge had set a deadline for my ex to accept. If he chose to drag the matter out longer, he would be financially responsible for all my legal fees as well. I was so angry at him for his treatment toward me and the length of time it took him to settle. At this point, we had been separated for more than a year. He wanted me to disappear. I wanted to move forward in my life. Even working full time, I could not afford to live on my own without his monthly support payment. He wanted out of this marriage and had moved on with his life.

On the evening of the deadline, my lawyer suggested I ask for a little more support as I would have to pay taxes on this amount. I asked for more than he had suggested. My lawyer said to me, "You are really upset. I am sure he would have wished he agreed on the original amount." My ex-husband reluctantly agreed on the higher amount of alimony. By that point, I did not really care how he felt. The most important person in my life was me—along with my family and friends who helped me through this painful part of my life.

Now that the separation agreement was over, I started to move forward in my life. I felt sad most of the time, but each day got easier. The feelings of rage and anger were slowly replaced with hope and encouragement. A person in the process of a divorce endures the same stages as one who has experienced the death of a loved one. Sometimes a divorce can be more difficult. I helped my mother as she experienced all the stages of recovery after my father's death. Unlike my husband, my dad had not chosen to leave my mother. Rejection is the most painful part of a divorce. Along with the help of a counsellor and reading many self-help books, I began to feel like a worthy person who deserved happiness and love.

To signify the end of my separation and marriage, I decided to get a tattoo. Work was slow that summer, so I left early one afternoon and drove my scooter to a reputable tattoo shop. I asked my friend Ed, better known as Uncle Buck, to meet me at the tattoo shop so he could assist me onto the table. The first thing he asked me was, "Does your mother know about this?"

I replied, "Absolutely not. Buck, when have I ever informed or asked my mother permission to do anything? She will find out soon enough."

The tattoo artist asked me to sign a consent form. He questioned my intentions and remarked, "Shelley, you seem a little delicate, are you sure you want this done?"

I looked him straight in the eye and said, "Honey, look at this scar on my leg. I have a fourteen-inch titanium rod along with six pins in my leg. Do you think a little tattoo is going to cause me any pain?" Uncle Buck started to laugh.

The tattoo artist looked at me and smiled, "I guess you are a lot tougher than you look." I loved the new tattoo on my ankle. It was a simple black artistic line with pink flowers dotted with white centers. It was tender for a few days. A week later, the tattoo had healed and looked fabulous.

I tried to become as independent as possible even if it meant travelling around the city without the use of special transportation. Some predicaments occurred during my excursions around our city. One evening, I was driving my wheelchair home from work on West Street when I experienced severe stomach pains. Once again, I called on my good friend, Uncle Buck, on my cell phone. I nervously spoke, "Uncle Buck, where are you? Do you think you could meet me at the mall? I need to get to a washroom or I am going to mess my pants!"

In his deep husky voice, Uncle Buck, replied, "No problem, I will meet you there."

As I proceeded down West Street hill over the highway underpass, the cramps were unbearable. I rang Uncle Buck one more time, "Buck, change of plans, I'm not going to make it to the mall. Can you meet me at Tim Horton's on West Street?"

In his deep voice he replied, "I'm on my way." It took me only three minutes to get to Timmy's, but those three minutes seemed like an eternity.

I entered the coffee shop, and Uncle Buck had already been waiting for me at the ladies washroom. My face was pasty white as sweat dripped profusely down my face. Buck looked at me, grabbed me in a bear hug, and yelled that a man was entering the female washroom. He opened the bathroom stall. Still in pain, I muttered, "Uncle Buck, can you close your eyes and help me get my pants down?" Buck was trying not to laugh as he fumbled to get my drawers down without looking and lowered me on to the toilet.

As he was leaving the bathroom, he yelled, "Let her rip, Shelley!" Two minutes later, I felt like a new woman. I do not know what I would have done if Uncle Buck had not come to my rescue. He was a true gentleman and a great friend.

Living life as a single woman was scary but liberating. Some days, I felt as though I had been given a get-out-of-jail-free card. In April 2005, after my separation agreement was complete, I purchased a condo unit not too far from my mother's house. When I first moved in to my new condo, I was terrified. My thoughts raced as I wondered if and how I could do this on my own. I worried about how I would get up in the night if I had to use the washroom. I could no longer get out of bed myself. My last home care worker left at 8:30 in the evening. I may have weak muscles, but God blessed me with a strong bladder. Wetting the bed or wearing adult diapers was not something I was ready to succumb to. I could visualize myself with a new loving boyfriend and trying to be real sexy saying something naughty like, "Honey, tear off my panties" instead of "Honey, tear off the straps of my hot, sexy diaper." I was not going there—not then and not for a long, long time!

One evening, my girlfriend Lori and I decided to go to a dance club. We were meeting a girlfriend at her apartment for a drink before we headed out. As we were driving to our destination, Lori and I spotted a vehicle driving erratically that swerved all over the road. Lori threw me her cell phone. "Shelley, dial 911 to call the police while I follow these intoxicated idiots." The driver almost hit a parked car on the side of the road. What if there had been children or adults walking along the road that evening? Lori tried to get the license plate number so I could pass the information on to the police officer. Luckily, the car we were following pulled into a local veteran's club. They must have seen us on their trail. The police told us to park somewhere in the parking lot and that they were on their way. When the police officers arrived, we pointed out the vehicle, and they headed over to check out the situation.

Lori and I started to wonder what was going to happen to this couple. It seemed like a long time before the officer knocked on our car window. Lori boldly started to question the officer, "How much alcohol have they had tonight?"

The policeman responded, "Neither one of these individuals have had a drink."

Lori started to laugh hysterically, "Are you sure? They clearly do not know how to drive!" She jokingly replied, "Well, if they are not drunk, they must be ninety years of age."

You should have seen the look on our faces when the officer responded, "Yes, ma'am, they are in their late eighties." The officers explained that this elderly couple had been frightened to death. The husband and wife were shaking when they spoke to the police officer about a car following them, so they pulled into this parking lot. It took every ounce of strength I had not to burst out in laughter and say, "Nice one, Lori."

We were quite embarrassed. We were even more embarrassed when Lori did not have her car insurance registration papers with her and was given a small fine. Lori and I had uncontrollable giggles all night. We still laugh about our good deed that went bad. We never would have forgiven ourselves if either one of these elderly individuals had had a heart attack! Our friends called us elder abusers that night.

Single life was kind of crazy. It reminded me of my old university days. The stronger the person I became, the more comfortable I felt alone. The thoughts of being in a relationship with a man seemed to be highly overrated. I remembered Aunt Louise asking me shortly after my separation, "What happened to that spunky young girl you used to be?" The old Shelley was starting to resurface.

A New Love

Three years after my legal separation, just as I established this newfound freedom, the unexpected happened. I was surfing the dating websites when I stumbled upon a site called Lava Life. My mother, being the worrier that she is, was convinced I was going to meet the homicidal maniac who would eventually end my life. Instead, I met a guy who called himself Mr. Tool Man. It all started with Jeff sending me a smile, so I sent him one back. There was one word in his profile that caught my attention. He described himself as witty—a word that I sometimes used to describe myself. We chatted online and found that we had been through similar life experiences and heartbreaks.

I think he wanted to ask me out, but I was hesitant and tried to push him away. I assumed that if I told him I was disabled and used a wheelchair, I would surely scare him away. Jeff was not frightened by my disability. He explained to me that his friend Al and his mother were in wheelchairs. Jeff was persistent. I remember him asking me if he needed to fill out an application to go out on a date with me. I responded, "Yes, you do."

Soon our conversations moved from the Internet to the telephone. I loved the sound of his voice and his adorable laugh. He was witty and funny. One evening, Jeff and I talked on the phone for three hours. Then he decided to bring coffee to me at my condo. Thinking back, I should never have agreed to meet Jeff the first time at my apartment. Although we had never met face-to-face, Jeff seemed to be trustworthy. By this point, we had been conversing for two months, so I felt confident Jeff was not a homicidal maniac. On that evening, I explained to Jeff that if I did not like his looks or demeanour, I would not allow him access to my building.

All the residents of my condo could see guests at the front door by turning their televisions to channel fifty-three. I was pleasantly surprised when I first saw Jeff at the entrance of my building. I decided to buzz him in after I told him my room number. We talked all night about our likes and dislikes, our families, and our love for animals. Jeff was funnier in person than over the telephone. I felt comfortable around him, unlike the awkwardness I felt with the few men I dated after my separation.

I was extremely tired at work the next day and went home early to catch up on sleep that I missed the night before. Around noon, my home care girl met me at my condo to assist me into bed instead of meeting me at work for my washroom break. That evening, Jeff and I spoke on the phone and arranged to go out for dinner the following weekend.

I was a little nervous about Jeff helping me in and out of my manual wheelchair as well as assisting me into and out of his van. He arrived at my condo around six o'clock that evening. Jeff pushed me in my manual wheelchair out to the condo parking lot. I tried to explain to Jeff that the best way to lift me out of my wheelchair was to lock his arms around my hips so he could get me into a standing position. Once I was upright, he could then carry me over the threshold on to the seat of his van.

Unbeknownst to me, Jeff decided he would do it his own way. Grabbing me around the waist, he lifted me up and then turned slightly to plant my butt on to the van seat. Little did he know that individuals with limb-girdle muscular dystrophy do not have the best upper body strength or balance. He also forgot that I had a fourteen-inch titanium rod inside my upper left leg (femur bone), which allowed for very little bending of the knee. When I landed on the seat of his van, my body resembled something similar to a stiff board. As I fell back across the front seat, Jeff fell on top of me. We starting laughing out loud and suddenly realized two elderly women in the parking lot were rather shocked when we heard them say, "Oh my!"

I thought, *This is going to be a long night.* I made the executive decision that it may be safer to pick up Chinese food and take it to my mother's house. I knew my sixty-seven-year-old mother could assist me out of the vehicle if Jeff had any difficulties. My mother and brother enjoyed meeting Jeff that evening, as well as eating the Chinese food. Our first official date ended more successfully than it had begun.

By May 2006, one month after we met in person, Jeff and I were spending a lot of time together. One morning, Jeff and I went out for breakfast with his friend Al, who was confined to a wheelchair. The first time I knew Jeff was a special person was when I saw him feeding Al. He had lost most of his hand movement due to the effects of cerebral palsy. My heart melted. I was definitely starting to fall head-over-heels in love with this man.

Our first trip to meet Jeff's family in Burlington was on Father's Day, one month later. While we were driving on the highway, I asked, "Did you tell your family about my disability and that I use a wheelchair?"

He replied with a grin, "No."

I was so freaked out that I asked Jeff to turn the car around. He told me not to worry; his family would accept me, disability and all. He was right. His family made me feel comfortable from the beginning.

Jeff and I visited my father's gravesite for the first time on Christmas Eve 2006. He laid a flower down as he knelt at my father's grave. It brought tears to my eyes. Jeff returned to the car quite upset. I asked him, "Why are you so upset? You never knew my dad." Jeff didn't say a word, but I knew what was on his mind. He was thinking about how difficult it would be when the time came to say good-bye to his parents.

When I first met Jeff, I was living in my own condo. I never thought I was strong enough to live on my own. With the help of my home care workers, I was able to do this. One Saturday morning, I had planned to go out for lunch with my friend Sylvia. She met me at my condo. As we started to walk down the hall, my leg gave out. I fell face-first on to the floor. Sylvia panicked. She helped me to a sitting position as my nose started bleeding. My face started to swell. Sylvia immediately telephoned Jeff at his townhouse and contacted my mother, explaining to each that I had fallen and needed medical attention.

By the time the three of us reached the walk-in clinic, my mouth had swollen four times its original size. Despite the look of my face, I only needed a couple of stitches underneath my chin. Jeff said, "Shelley, do not look at yourself in the mirror." Of course, my curiosity got the better of me; I snuck a peek. I truly looked like a monster or an alien. The swelling was so bad that I couldn't talk. For the first time in my life, I was completely silent.

It was exactly a week later when my "old face" reappeared. I was sitting up in bed one morning just after one of my home care workers arrived. I felt something running down the back of my throat. I immediately yelled for a Kleenex as my nose started to bleed. My home care worker yelled, "Oh no! Shelley, don't move." She ran for a towel. The blood was pouring out so fast from my nose that it soaked the towel in minutes. The bedsheets and my nightshirt were covered in blood. Then I started to panic. My worker called her boss, who was a registered nurse. She instructed her to pinch my nose as hard as she could. When that did not stem the flow of blood, she instructed us to call 911.

The ambulance drivers arrived at the condo quite quickly. By then, I had started spitting up large jelly-like amoebas. Frightened, I asked the driver, "Am I going to be okay?" They explained that the blood was starting to clot. While this was a good sign, I had not planned to spend my Saturday vomiting huge blood clots. I instructed my home care girl to contact my mother and Jeff and ask them to meet us at the hospital ER department.

After I was brought to the ER, the doctors could not determine where the blood was coming from. The doctor would have preferred to cauterize the area, but the bleeding refused to stop, making it impossible to perform the procedure. My mother and Jeff remained in the treatment room with me. The doctors decided to freeze my nose and pack it. Jeff and my mother left the room while the doctor treated me. When they returned, the first comment from Jeff's mouth was, "If I knew they were going to put a tampon up your nose, I could have saved you a trip to the hospital and done this myself." I wanted to cry, but all I could do was laugh with him. I was released from the hospital shortly after the doctor finished the treatment.

I stayed at my mother's house for the weekend so she could spoil me with TLC since Jeff was busy working on something at his townhouse. Two hours later, the freezing wore off. The pain was excruciating. Think of your worst sinus headache and multiply the pain by ten times. This was the longest forty-eight hours of my life. I don't know why bad things happen to good people. Maybe God knew that I could handle it. I had two choices: I could cry and feel sorry for myself, or I could laugh about it and move on. With only one life and one body, I learned to make the best of what was given to me.

Laughter became a big part of my life, thanks to Jeff. He was great at entertaining my home care workers. One evening, my personal support worker was in my condo bedroom. She asked me what pyjamas I wanted to wear. Jeff's voice yelled down from the living room, "Don't bother putting any on her—it will save me some time later!" She was quite surprised.

I rolled my eyes and said, "Have you met my boyfriend, Jeff?"

The condo building where I resided was well kept. Most of the tenants were retired individuals. I met a lot of wonderful, caring people. Most tenants knew me as the young woman in the wheelchair. I remember one tenant who approached me in the lobby. After we introduced ourselves, I couldn't believe what she said to me. "Shelley, you are too pretty to be in a wheelchair!" Taken aback, I wondered if I should feel flattered by this statement. I wasn't sure how to respond so I simply smiled at her.

Later that evening, I told Jeff what this tenant had said and then added, "Can you imagine if I was unsightly and disabled?" Life was difficult enough living with muscular dystrophy. Maybe disabled individuals are not supposed to be attractive. I have always cared about my appearance; I love fashion and am very conscientious about my figure. It has always been important for me to eat healthy and get plenty of rest. Maintaining my weight has always been imperative so I can continue to walk for as long as possible. My physical looks have no relation to my disability. My mother is extremely attractive. I credit her for my personal appearance and feel truly blessed that I inherited some of her genes. I feel flattered that people admire my outer beauty, but my truly authentic inner beauty defines the real me—kindhearted, caring, and sincere.

One evening, Jeff came to my condo and surprised me with a lovely bouquet of flowers. What a sweetheart. I was already in my pyjamas and sitting in bed when he handed me the flowers. I lowered my face to smell their fragrance when a large moth flew out and smacked me in the face. "Jeff," I screamed. "Please grab this moth and get it out of here—get it, get it." My cat, Sophie, watched the moth's every move.

Jeff was laughing when he said, "Shelley, if I was you, I would shut your mouth before the moth ends up in it." Jeff found the broom, and the poor moth met its demise. Normally, Jeff would have trapped the insect and set it free outside. We both have big hearts, even for those ugly critters.

The first Christmas Jeff and I spent together, he bought me an adorable male cockapoo. As the puppy was the colour of my favourite Christmas cocktail, Bailey's Irish Cream, I named him Bailey.

Three months later, in February 2007, Jeff and I purchased our first home together. By mid-April, most of our personal belongings had been unpacked. Bailey, and Jeff's twelve-year-old yellow lab, Cindy, took the move in stride. Given that the house we purchased was on a busy street, I made the decision to give Sophie to my mother since she lived on a quiet street. I arrived home from work on our local wheelchair transit bus. One of my young, home care workers, Jaclyn, was waiting for me. The driver, George, noticed that the front bedroom window was broken. He did not want to worry us, so he decided to look in the window to see if a ball had been thrown into it. I immediately asked him, "Are there some of my watercolour paintings on the bed?"

George replied, "Yes, there is. It doesn't look like anything is out of place."

Just as a precaution, George escorted Jaclyn and me through the garage entrance into the house. He glanced around and said everything looked fine. George was just about to leave as Jaclyn went down to open the bedroom door and assess the clutter of broken glass. All of a sudden, the most horrific scream came out of her mouth. If Jaclyn had been auditioning for the loudest scream in a horror movie, she definitely would have been awarded the part. Shaking and stuttering, Jaclyn tried to explain what she saw.

George ran down to the bedroom and yelled, "Holy shit!" A huge turkey vulture spread its wings—a span of four feet—and flew out the window that he had broken on his entrance to the bedroom. We were thankful Cindy and Bailey were locked in the kitchen. Cindy would have torn the intruder apart. The turkey vulture stayed long enough to take a huge dump on our bedroom floor. Jeff could not leave work, so my brother-in-law, Jim, had the honour of cleaning the sharp glass and stinky mess.

My aunt and uncle lived two doors down. They too were amazed that a large bird had flown through our window. We could not find any part of the turkey vulture after it vacated our premises. My uncle jokingly commented that he thought he would have a dead bird to cook for Easter dinner the following week. Jeff's friend Troy came over to insert a board to replace the window until we could get a new piece of glass. The adage states: when a bird defecates on you, it's good luck. Does anyone know if the same scenario applies when a bird flies through your house window and leaves a large stinky mess?

A couple days later, Troy installed a new piece of glass in the bedroom window. Jeff's birthday was the following day, so we asked our families to come over to celebrate. Before Troy left, he left a sign on our front yard that included a picture of a target's bull's-eye and the words: *Turkey Shoot, Sunday between 2:00–4:00 p.m.* He also left a note on our front door: *All turkeys please enter through the front door.* Our relatives laughed about our story and these signs! I know the other wheelchair transit drivers laughed hysterically when George acted out the events that occurred that evening.

Living with a disabled person can be difficult at times. The assistance from my personal support workers allowed Jeff to be my partner and not a caretaker. I am so thankful that free home health care is available in Canada.

When my disability became unmanageable for me to transfer out of bed on my own or dress myself, I required the help of home health care workers through a community care access center that is operated through the Ontario government. When I first started using home health care services, I was allocated three hours of service a day through the CCAC system. Now I manage my care through a program called Direct Funding. For those who live with a disability and require more personal home care hours than a regular agency can provide, Direct Funding may be needed. The option of private home care may be feasible when more hours are needed.

When I first applied for Direct Funding, I was asked to note my personal needs in time allotments. This made it easier to assess the time I required for assistance. I was approved for four hours of service per day for seven days a week. My personal support workers assist me with showering, toiletry needs, getting dressed, meal preparation, house cleaning, transferring from one position to another, shopping for the groceries, and bedtime. As my own manager, I hire, manage, keep track of my payroll hours, and submit these hours to a payroll agent who calculates the pay. I write checks twice a month for my workers. I respect my workers and appreciate their assistance each and every day. Living with muscular dystrophy or any other neuromuscular disease does not mean that you cannot live on your own. With the assistance of health care, Jeff does not have the sole burden of helping me with the daily tasks of living.

Jeff takes pride in entertaining—or should I say, teasing—my caregivers. One morning, he came out of the shower with a towel wrapped around his waist. I was quite surprised because Jeff usually dressed in the bathroom after his shower. This particular home care aide was quite shy. Jeff walked by her and dropped his towel. Her face turned beet red. Jeff had a pair of rolled up pants on underneath the towel. Laughing hysterically, he managed to say, "I didn't see you turn away when the towel fell!" He always made the caregivers laugh even when he embarrassed them.

My finances were pretty limited when we moved into our home, so I used special transportation to get to most of my destinations. When the weather was warmer, I used my scooter to get across the city just to save a couple of dollars. It was also a great way to catch a nice tan.

One afternoon, I was running late for a hair appointment. Knowing I had to make up for some lost time, I turned my electric scooter on high.

A voice in my head said, *Shelley, hold on to both handlebars.* I wish I had listened to that voice. I literally started to fly down one of the largest hills in our city, but I hadn't envisioned the rut in the sidewalk. Holding on with one hand, my upper body flew forward, pushing on the hand controls. I was driving erratically now. I knew I was in trouble. I didn't have the strength to push myself back in the upright position, especially moving with a downward force. As I looked down a flight of stairs at the end of the hill, I closed my eyes and said a prayer, "God, I do not want to die today." Someone must have been watching over me. I hit the railing on the staircase and my scooter stopped dead. Then it tipped over, and I smashed my head on the sidewalk.

Several people stopped to assist me. One man said, "Remain calm. An ambulance is on the way." He asked me my name and if I knew what day it was. How embarrassing! The gentleman picked me up and put me on to my scooter. My head hurt so badly.

Once I got my bearings, the first thing I thought about was my hair appointment. The crowd stared in astonishment as I prepared to drive away. Was I gutsy or just plain stupid? In either case, I turned to the crowd and said, "Thank you for all your help. I have a hair appointment to attend." The crowd watched in astonishment as I drove away. This was neither the first nor the last blow to my head. This time, however, I winced every time my hairdresser ran the comb through my hair. I knew I had a concussion. Jeff had to wake me up every two hours that night. They say what doesn't kill you makes you stronger.

Jeff and I experienced tough times over the last couple of years. We both come from broken marriages and spousal problems. Jeff has three children from his first marriage. He and his ex-wife had an older boy and two younger girls. Unfortunately, Jeff has not had the opportunity to get to know his children as well as he would have liked. Every Saturday, he drives forty-five minutes to visit two of his children, the eldest boy and his youngest daughter.

It truly breaks my heart that some former spouses put their agendas ahead of their children's needs. A lot of negative talk about Dad and brainwashing by his ex has caused problems between Jeff and his children. His wife was the one who wanted to terminate the marriage. Jeff has never missed a child support or alimony payment. Why do some women feel entitled to sit at home while their former spouses work in order to support them? Before Jeff and his wife met, she worked two jobs while living in England with her parents. Once she travelled to Canada to spend the summers with her aunt and uncle, she and Jeff started hanging out. Two years later, they were married. Once she officially moved to Canada and was married, she worked full time for several months. Jeff always encouraged his wife to go out and work full time before the children were born. Once the two eldest children were in school full time, he wanted her to find part-time employment, since she was a seamstress by trade. It is extremely difficult to raise a family on one income. His wife did not seem to care that Jeff was extremely frustrated by her choice to stay home.

I truly believe Jeff and I were destined to meet. He has been my rock. Hopefully, I can help him deal with the upcoming challenges we will face regarding his children. Since Jeff's eldest son turned eighteen, Mom has not stopped him from spending more time with his father. I do not believe Jeff and his middle daughter can develop a meaningful relationship, but I hope I am wrong. I believe the emotional damage has been too severe. Some children will internalize and pity the parent they live with because he or she is unhappy and lonely. These children justify and rationalize the insecure parent's actions. For example, the mom tells her children that their dad was a horrible husband and parent during their marriage. This misinformation usually destroys the children's relationship and trust they share with their father.

Everything seemed to be going well in our relationship. Unfortunately, I was working in a dead-end job for a call center. I was unhappy but did not have the nerve to quit my job until I could find another one. One Friday evening in August 2008, Sherry, my home care giver walked with me to the kitchen. I thought I had reached the kitchen counter and asked her to let go. Evidently, I didn't have the counter and toppled head-over-heels and fell hard on the kitchen floor.

I immediately started screaming. I had felt this kind of pain once before. My head was rocking back and forth, the same action that occurred when I broke my leg four years earlier. Sherry called my mother and Uncle Buck to come over to my house. I was in a lot of pain and felt safer with more people around to get me into a more comfortable position. Sherry and my mother made the decision to call an ambulance. Jeff was at work when he was notified that I had fallen and was being transported by ambulance to the hospital's emergency department. Jeff left work and quickly drove to the hospital where we both patiently waited for the doctor.

I remember that evening all too well. Jeff was great and kept my mind off the pain. So many different incidents happened that night. When they brought me into the ER, the nurse who took my personal information asked me why I had come into the ER on a stretcher. I explained that I had a mild form of muscular dystrophy and was unable to hop on one leg. Her reply was, "You have muscular dystrophy and are forty-four years old? I am surprised you are still alive!" What a pleasant comment coming from one of health care's finest. I was shocked she said this to me.

The night had just begun. A young man was brought in by the police. He had inserted a bag of cocaine up his gluteus maximus. That same nurse responded to the gentleman with the narcotics, "Why did you go and do a thing like that?" Jeff and I tried to hold back our laughter. Jeff was all too eager to ask which doctor had to go digging for the cocaine. I remember the medical student laughing as he pointed to the female doctor on call. The medical student was amused by Jeff's comment and referred to Jeff as this hilarious guy who should be a comedian.

Another police officer brought in several fingers from a young woman who had a fight with her boyfriend; he had slammed her hand in the car door. I believe three of her fingers were amputated. I remember Jeff saying to me, "This is better than Friday night television." The doctor X-rayed my leg and said it was badly sprained. I took a few days off work since I could not put any weight on my leg.

A painful week passed as I struggled to put weight on my leg. I returned to the walk-in clinic where the physician on call arranged for me to see an orthopaedic surgeon. The following week I had a bone scan, which showed that my leg was broken with a crack in my tibia plateau underneath my left knee. The doctor remarked that I was fortunate not to have damaged it further by walking on it. I knew it was more than a sprain. Living with muscular dystrophy is not easy. This was the second broken leg in five years. I briefly considered give up walking completely. While the fear of falling was overwhelming, the thought of never walking again frightened me more.

Back to School—A Career Change

I was absent from work for approximately eight weeks. When it was time to return to my place of employment, I could not cope mentally with the idea of returning to my job. My doctor wrote a note stating that I would not be returning to this job but was able to find different employment. I met with a few counsellors. I have always been interested in the medical profession. After spending so much time in the hospital, I had a revelation. "Jeff, I feel comfortable in a medical setting." I made the decision to take a medical administration course at a local college in town.

The course was ten months in duration. I loved learning about the body systems, medical terminology, and medical transcription. I studied a minimum of three hours a day. Around November 2008, our local wheelchair transportation services went on strike. Thankfully, the college I attended was only six blocks away from our home. I was determined to get to class every day even if the weather was not cooperative.

In Canada, the months of November through March are extremely cold. Some days, the snow was heavy, but a little snow and ice never hurt anyone. My home care attendants bundled me up—including long johns underneath the mandatory scrubs we had to wear. I wore a heavy down-filled coat, hat, scarf, and mittens. A plastic bag covered my wheelchair control pad. Jeff could hear me laughing as I drove down the road and fishtailed as I tried to drive in somewhat of a straight direction while my wheelchair struggled to get traction.

When the weather was at its worst, Jeff offered to drive me to school before he left for work. I refused his offer every time. Driving my wheelchair in the winter was a little crazy and dangerous, but it was fun. I ended up in a snow bank on only three occasions. Usually someone saw me struggling with a panicked look on my face and rescued me from the snow bank. I never missed a day of school during those ten months.

During the Christmas holidays in 2008, Jeff's fourteen-year-old yellow lab, Cindy, collapsed on the floor. I think she was having a seizure, as she was shaking uncontrollably. A few months earlier, the vet ran a series of blood tests. Her blood work had shown an abnormally high level of steroids. Our veterinarian diagnosed her with Cushing's disease. Jeff did not want to put her through any more tests. As long as Cindy wasn't in any pain and was eating, we decided to leave things alone.

Jeff rushed Cindy to the vet clinic after she collapsed. They kept her overnight to monitor her progress. When Jeff called the vet the next morning, the news was not good. Cindy had suffered a stroke and was not able to move the back half of her body. Jeff began to cry. Cindy had been with Jeff through his painful divorce. She was more loving and loyal to him than his wife had been. He looked at me, and we cried. We knew it was her time. Jeff took our little dog Bailey with him to say good-bye to his buddy. Wow, that was such a hard day. The experience brought back memories of when I had to put my little Ebony down. I cried so much and so loud that there wasn't a dry eye at the clinic that day.

Original watercolour Cindy by Shelley Tudin

Back to the Hospital

As part of the medical administration course, all students had to complete a five-week placement at a medical facility to successfully complete the course. I worked at a local medical clinic where my doctor had his practice. Things were working out well for me at this clinic. I was just about to complete my fourth week of placement on June 25, 2009, when I had yet another devastating fall. I had tumbled sideways coming out of the bathroom in our bedroom and landed on my right hip. Immediately, I knew something was broken. Jeff called the ambulance. My fears came true once again. I snapped the neck of my right femur just before the hip socket. I couldn't help thinking, *I can't go through this again—surgery and then weeks of rehab.* The tears came flooding down my cheeks. This day happened to be more memorable than I could have imagined and put things in perspective. Michael Jackson and Farrah Fawcett passed away that day. Thankfully, I had only broken my right hip and was still alive and breathing.

A family member called the clinic where I was completing my placement to inform them about the fall and broken right hip. One of my fellow students came to visit me in the hospital. She told me that when an announcement was made to the staff regarding my unfortunate accident tears rolled down many of their faces. Everyone felt bad for me, but it made me feel special that I had made an impact on them in four short weeks.

After ten days on the surgical ward, I was transferred to the rehab floor for therapy. Some of those old memories and insecurities from the first broken femur began to surface. Unlike my first husband, Jeff was emotionally present for me. He made me laugh when all I wanted to do was cry. Once again, I was spending the summer in the hospital. I just wanted to get out of the hospital and look for employment. I missed Jeff, Bailey, and our cat, Sienna.

For me, being a patient in a hospital for a lengthy amount of time is difficult. Depending on another person twenty-four hours a day is extremely frustrating. Ringing a bell to get a nurse to assist you is very humbling. For the most part, the medical staff was quite accommodating. Some of the younger nurses seemed more caring and patient.

One evening, I rang the bell around 11:00 p.m. I had to go to the bathroom. Once the bell was rung, a nurse asked over the intercom what was needed. I don't know why they wouldn't come down to assist you. Being in pain and taking a lot of narcotics did not help the situation. Sometimes I felt like saying, "I rang the bell just to piss you off." What did they think I wanted? A few minutes later, the nurse arrived at my bedside. I explained to her that I had to go the bathroom. She rudely replied, "The other nurse was down here at 9:30 p.m. for your washroom break."

I responded, "No, she brought me a warm blanket. I haven't been to the bathroom since 7:00 p.m." She started arguing with me as if I didn't recall my evening. Now I was really mad.

Miserably I responded, "Get the damn bed pan and put it under my butt now, or I will wet the bed and give you something to really complain about!" She looked at me in astonishment. I don't recall having a problem with her after that night.

Surgery is required for a major broken bone, and it is necessary to take pain medication to get through the rehabilitation process. The medication takes the edge off the pain; however, the side effects of these narcotics are extremely uncomfortable. By the second week in rehab, the pain of constipation seemed worse than the pain from the broken bone and surgery. My mother was visiting one evening when I was in the bathroom crying because I was not able to relieve myself. Even though we kept ringing the help button, not one of the nurses responded. I decided to take matters into my own hands and asked my mother to hand me a glove.

By the morning, my favourite male nurse pumped me full of orange liquid as I drank a bottle of water. I told him what had happened the night before. He explained, "You should never attempt to do that again. It is extremely dangerous. You could tear the inner lining, but at least you were smart enough to wear a glove." Wow, the stomach cramps came on so intensely. My nurse got me on a travelling commode and raced me to the bathroom. He yelled, "Let her rip, Shelley." This was the second time in my life I heard that phrase. I literally felt like I was in labour. I think the entire floor heard me yell. This event was so traumatic that I stopped taking ninety percent of my pain medication. I was edgy, but I wasn't ever going to go through that experience again.

While I was on the rehab floor, I met a young man named Rick. He had told me that he had been in the hospital for a year and a half. When we met outside on the patio on the second floor of the hospital, I realized who Rick was. His parents lived one block from my parents' home. Even though I knew of him and his family, I never really knew him personally. We both had grown up in the same neighbourhood.

Rick explained to me that he suffered from multiple sclerosis. He had gone to bed Christmas Eve 2007, and when he awoke, he could not feel his legs or feet. He'd had a severe MS attack and was rushed up to the hospital. Since multiple sclerosis affects the immune system, Rick developed a severe bladder infection, which later turned into renal failure. Once he made it through the initial couple of months, Rick was able to transfer himself in and out of bed with a transfer board. Unfortunately, he got a bed sore. This bed sore became infected and almost tunnelled to the bone. From this point on, Rick was bedridden until the wound started to heal.

Rick and I have a lot in common. His wife left him when he started to show more signs of his disease. After graduating from McGill University in Montreal, he was accepted into law school in North Dakota. This was also where he met and fell in love with his wife. They were married for almost eight years. His wife and my ex-husband must have had the same seven-year itch. Once she asked for a divorce, Rick returned to Canada to live with his parents. Apparently, the "in sickness and in health" marital vows do not mean anything to some when push comes to shove.

Rick spent two years preparing so he could take the Canadian bar exam. After passing the bar, he worked for a law firm in Brantford for a year before becoming ill. I think of all the time Rick had spent in school to practice law. He had such a great attitude about life. I could not imagine spending all that time in a hospital. I truly look up to Rick for inspiration when I get down or start feeling sorry for myself. I think I truly broke my hip to meet and become friends with Rick. Our friendship made those five weeks in rehab bearable. When I returned home from the hospital, I had to wait another month to finish my placement at the clinic where I originally started.

My overall average for the year was 98.9 percent, one of the highest overall averages for the entire 2008–2009 school year. I thank my dear love,

Jeff, for all his support during this academic year. Jeff's encouragement was the most determining factor that allowed me to make this career change.

Toward the end of July 2009, we received a call from Jeff's' older sister, Debbie, that their father, Sylvester, had been admitted into the hospital with chest pains. He had suffered a mild heart attack years before when his wife, Muriel's, health was failing due to Alzheimer's disease. Sylvester was truly an inspirational man. He was diagnosed with Parkinson's disease in 2002. Despite his own health issues, when Muriel became ill with Alzheimer's disease, Sylvester assisted his wife with all the tasks of daily living at home until 2003, when he could no longer take care of her. She was hospitalized, but Sylvester visited her faithfully each and every day.

Jeff and his father shared the same love and passion of flying. Jeff's dad had been an aircraft mechanic during the Second World War. Sylvester and Jeff loved to fly remote control planes. They spent hours together flying planes at their club field in Burlington, Ontario. Jeff and his father spent time flying on Saturday afternoon and then headed to the hospital to visit Muriel. The family took turns visiting their mom so their father could have a break in the evenings.

When Muriel passed away in September 2008, Sylvester seemed so lonely without his dear loving wife. He put up a brave front, but I think his body was tiring. Every summer, Jeff took his father to visit his sister, Donna, and her husband, Frank's, cottage to enjoy some time at the lake in northern Ontario. Donna and Frank had been building their cottage from the foundation up. Jeff and his father helped build some of this cottage.

After Debbie informed Jeff about Sylvester's admittance into the hospital, Jeff called the hospital every day to see how his father was doing. The nurse on the Coronary Care Unit informed Jeff that his father's condition was improving and that he would be moved from the ward the following morning. Jeff asked the nurse to let his father know that he would be there Saturday to see him.

That same evening, around 11:30 p.m., Debbie called us and was very upset. I immediately knew something was wrong. She informed Jeff that their father had passed away. He went into tachycardia and had a massive heart attack. I began to cry uncontrollably. Jeff was quiet; I knew he was in shock. Since Jeff was disoriented and I was still in a lot of pain from the hip fracture, I immediately called my mother to come over to help me get dressed. Jeff and I needed to travel to Burlington to get to the hospital. I felt so bad for Jeff. He worked long hours as a mechanic, and I knew he felt guilty that he had not visited his father that week. The next few days were tough. I remember how terrible I felt when my father passed away. Jeff had now lost both of his parents in fewer than two years.

Jeff cried on and off for months. I remember offering him a lot of hugs every time he cried. I told him it was okay and healthy for him to let his emotions out. Jeff and I grew closer as we experienced these difficult times together.

Original Watercolour of Muriel and Sylvester, 2009 by Shelley Tudin

Scared to Death—Finding Employment from a Wheelchair

After graduation, I was extremely frustrated looking for employment again. Most of my fellow students had found work in the medical field. I was annoyed that I had not been hired for any of the positions I applied for. My qualifications were current, and I was being interviewed for positions.

I did not want to believe that I wasn't hired because of the electric wheelchair I used. Why are so many people frightened to hire disabled individuals? The managers who conducted the interviews had the same level of education I had. I visited my friend Rick a couple times a week at the hospital. He kept my spirits high as I received rejection after rejection. I began to doubt my abilities. My attitude began to change when I ran into one of my former classmates from the medical administration course that had landed a job at our local hospital. She assured me that something would come along and commented, "Shelley, you were the smartest girl in our class. Everyone in the class voted for you for valedictorian." That comment offered me inspiration and hope that I would obtain successful employment.

In November 2009, I was selected from two hundred applicants to work at an Ontario medical clinic. The clinic had interviewed five applicants and selected me. I was so excited. It was as though I had won the lottery. For the first time in my life, I had a job that I was proud of and had worked hard to achieve—all on my own. My insecurities and rejections did not seem to matter now. Jeff was proud and excited for me. I think I called everyone with the good news. My family and friends were especially happy. At last, I had a great job that paid good wages and offered great benefits and a pension. Although this employment opportunity was for a limited contract term, I was hopeful the job may become a permanent position or lead me in the direction toward future medical job opportunities.

I loved working for this organization. Although I was hired for three different departments, I accepted this position to gain experience and knowledge regarding the policies and procedures of running a medical clinic. I was nervous and overwhelmed those first few months. Since many employers have not given me, a physically challenged person, the opportunity to work for their organization, I wanted to work harder and achieve more than a nondisabled worker. The expectations I placed on myself were far greater than the expectations that others placed on me.

The clinic physician and registered nurse were extremely patient with me during those first few months of employment. I was responsible for scheduling appointments for the physician, the nurse, and the massage therapist, as well as checking in arriving patients, faxing specialist referrals, and entering various incoming clinical, operative, and admission reports into medical software. Financially, I was in charge of Ontario Health Insurance Plan billing, daily summary and accounts receivable reports. I was also responsible for collecting currency for missed appointments and billing insurance companies for international students.

The other two departments were not as labour intensive but the workload for all three departments was heavy. Even though this position was challenging, I loved the students and my fellow coworkers. I found it difficult to complete all the necessary daily tasks required as the number of students at this institution increased. Unfortunately, my intellect was capable of soaking up so much more information; however, my body and weak muscles could not move as quickly as I would have liked.

In my opinion, due to the heavy workload, it was not humanly possible for me to complete a day's work in the time permitted—and definitely not possible for a person with muscular dystrophy who worked from a wheelchair.

Finding a good-paying job for those who are physically disabled is difficult. In Canada, legislation has mandated that all new buildings become barrier free for those using wheelchairs. An electronic button to open a door seems simple, but many businesses do not have these in place. Larger metropolitan cities such as Toronto, Ottawa, and Hamilton have more employment opportunities for persons with disabilities. The Ontario government has employment programs to assist persons with disabilities in finding employment in their fields. Employers still have a long way to go to fully grasp and understand what disabled people in the workforce require; however, organizations are becoming more aware of and accepting disabled individuals as part of their work environment. Physical barriers in the workplace are improving, but persons with disabilities also require more than an ergonomically correct workstation. Many of us need more time to complete tasks since our mobility is impaired, especially those people living with limb-girdle muscular dystrophy. The best way to describe the feeling of weak muscles and fatigue—it's similar to an able-bodied person strapping fifty-pound weights on their arms, legs, shoulders, and hips before performing a typical desk job as quickly as their nondisabled coworkers. This would not be any easy task.

Life seemed to be falling into place. I loved my job, coworkers, and students at the facility. Jeff seemed more relaxed now that he didn't have the sole burden of all the home finances. He had been supporting his former wife and children for more than ten years.

In early December 2009, two weeks after I obtained employment, Jeff seemed to be acting strange. He was excited about something—like a kid in a candy store anticipating something wonderful. On Christmas Eve morning, I had just showered, put my pajama's back on, and went out to the living room. Jeff had to work that day but would be home early. He walked out in the living room and presented me with a little white box. I wondered, *Is that what I think it is?* I slowly opened the box and was a bit shocked to see that it was a pair of diamond earrings. I didn't want to seem ungrateful.

Jeff said, "Honey, you didn't think I was going to buy you a diamond ring, did you?" I couldn't really respond to that comment. My home care girl Linda was there that morning. She left after I opened the box. I thought she left because there was not going to be an engagement announcement.

I was surprised when Jeff came out with a second box. My heart started to pound. Jeff had a big grin on his face. He never ceased to amaze me. The second box held a beautiful diamond ring. I had tears in my eyes. The funny thing was that he never really asked me to marry him. All he said was, "Do you want to, honey?"

I was about to take another leap of faith and get married for the second time. "Of course, I will marry you," I replied.

That's my Jeff. We went to my family's Christmas Eve party that evening. I showed everyone my ring. I was excited to have a second chance at love and marriage. This time, I felt like I was marrying my best friend.

Around Valentine's Day in 2010, Jeff and I browsed the Internet on a free website for selling vehicles, appliances, animals, and household items. We found an ad posted by a family who needed to sell their eleven-month-old, forty-seven pound, male, apricot cockapoo. The following day, after contacting the family, Jeff decided to take Bailey with him to meet the owners and the dog. Without hesitation, he purchased this beautiful puppy named Maxwell. The owners did not have the time to spend with him since their young son had recently become terminally ill. Maxwell blended in with our family quite nicely although he was quite rambunctious.

Jeff and I love our pets as if they were our children. Although we have no children together, Maxwell and Bailey, and our cat, Sienna, give us unconditional love and keep us extremely busy.

In April 2010, the school year was starting to wind down. The students wrote final exams in the beginning of April and ended around Easter weekend. Our health clinic closed down for the summer months as only a minimal number of students stayed on for the spring and summer terms. The work hours for my position were reduced during the months of May through August. It was nice to work three days a week during the warm months. I had a lot of preparation and creative ideas to complete before our August wedding in Kingsville, Ontario.

Our Beachfront Wedding

"It only takes a moment to say I love you, but it will take a lifetime to show you how much."

Jeff and I decided to marry the following summer. Since we had been together, Jeff and I loved visiting Aunt Josey and Uncle Harry's beachfront home. It was only fitting to hold our wedding in Kingsville, Ontario, a location we both adored. We started booking the caterers, the minister, the tent, etc., in early February. We didn't want anything too large since we were paying for the event.

Jeff and I travelled to Kingsville on August 5, 2010. We helped my aunt and uncle and their best friends as they spent many hours getting ready for the big event. The wedding party arrived on a Friday. My good friend Melissa and her boyfriend, Jim, were wonderful in helping us prepare for the big day. I met Melissa in 2004 when she worked for a home care agency in Brantford. She continued to work as my home care worker when I moved into my own condo. She was a great support for me while I was dealing with the emotional ups and downs after my ex-husband and I separated. We have shared a lot of laughs. The night before the wedding, Melissa, Jim, and I were driving back to the hotel in Leamington when a song started to play on the radio, "Single Ladies (Put a Ring on It)" by Beyoncé. Jim cranked the volume as he said to me, "Sing it, Shell, this is your last night as a single girl."

On August 7, 2010, I married my best friend, the one I live with, laugh with, and love. The day and location were absolutely beautiful. The ceremony was outside on the front deck with Lake Erie in the background. It was so romantic having a beachfront wedding. Even though the sun was shining, a warm southern breeze kept our guests comfortable. I wore a sleeveless off-white wedding dress with a crisscrossed chiffon pattern in the back. My sister, Michele, and my close friend Stephanie, the bridesmaids, wore short, soft sky-blue satin cocktail dresses. Our bouquets were composed of ivory roses with a hint of greenery, giving a beautiful scented fragrance. We could hear the waves of Lake Erie in the background. Jeff and his best man Troy, and groomsman and brother-in-law, Jim, wore long-sleeved, ivory dress shirts with paisley ties and black dress pants.

Jeff and Shelley's August 7, 2010, wedding

I was determined to walk down the aisle. Muscular dystrophy and three broken legs would not stop me from joining my future husband. I had asked Jim, my brother-in-law, to accompany me. I know my father would have approved of this decision. Jim had spoken the last words to my father before he passed. Jim had also provided great support to me after my separation. I could not imagine asking anyone else. I know know my father, John, as well as Jeff's father, Sylvester, and mother, Muriel, were looking down and smiling on us.

The music started to play. We had selected "This I Promise You" by Ronan Keating. This is one of the most beautiful songs I have ever heard. Wow, what a long walk. Approximately halfway to my destination, I stopped and said to everyone, "Good thing I picked a long song!" Everyone chuckled. One step at a time, my eyes filled with tears, Jim and I finally reached the altar. I was overcome with emotion. All the heartache and pain during the last six years was behind me.

After the minister pronounced us man and wife, he added, "Jeff, you may now kiss your wife." Jeff leaned over to kiss me just as I began to lose my balance. Thankfully, my girlfriend's husband, Trevor, was right there waiting with a manual wheelchair. During the ceremony, Jeff's two nieces Stephanie and Katie recited a love poem.

The wedding ceremony

Our reception was held under a large tent with seventy-five of our closest friends and family members. Jeff's twin brother, Greg, was the master of ceremonies. White linens draped the round tables, and soft blue hydrangeas in glass vases accented the tables. The red and white wines on the tables were brewed with love by my sister, Michele, and her husband, Jim. As a token of our appreciation, we gave our guests a chocolate truffle and a small bottle of blush wine. Each bottle had a custom-stamped verse: "It only takes a moment to say I love you, but it will take a lifetime to show you how much."

The dinner was catered by Calasanti's, an Italian company well known in southern Ontario. Each table had a special task to accomplish to see the bride and groom kiss. The funniest task was given to a table of my home care workers.

The table setting at dinner

The couples had to perform their task in front of the head table. Nicole and Melissa were blindfolded. The gentlemen rolled up their pants. Nicole and Melissa had to identify the legs belonging to their mate. Roger and Jim decided to intertwine their legs so the girls became really confused when they started to feel the legs. Our guests laughed hysterically.

Melissa insisted Jeff and I deliver an extra special kiss due to the "humiliation and embarrassment" in the task of identifying her husband's legs. Jeff jumped on my wheelchair, straddling me, and planted a big, wet kiss on my mouth. Unfortunately, he forgot that he detailed the wheelchair with Armor All and slid off the chair, pulling a groin muscle in the process. If Jeff had accidentally hit the on switch on my wheelchair, he would have driven us into the head table or backed us into the tent post. What a crazy man! It's been four years, and Jeff still continues to make me laugh every day.

Our family and friends danced the night away under the stars on the deck facing Lake Erie. The music was graciously downloaded by my niece Niana. Our guests had a great time with our dear friend and ever-so-entertaining bartender Uncle Buck.

Our wedding bartender, Uncle Buck

After the weekend, Jeff and I drove away from my aunt and uncle's home very slowly. We listened to the wedding ceremony music in the car. Jeff and I both started to cry; it was such a happy, emotional ceremony. The truth is we are both sappy!

We went up north for a couple of days to relax at the Nottawasaga Inn. Since the university shut down at Christmas, Jeff had booked holidays for a week in December and two weeks in January to go on our official honeymoon at that time.

Shelley in the gardens at the Nottawasaga Resort, August 2010

Fall—A Time for Change

I returned back to work after a week of vacation in August. When September hit, along with my coworkers, I was extremely busy helping new students adjust to college life. If God could have granted me one wish—I would have asked him to cure me so I would no longer have to struggle with the challenges living with limb-girdle muscular dystrophy. The workload was growing, but I could not keep afloat. The contract came to an end.

I appreciate everything the doctor did for me and truly thank her from the bottom of my heart. She was a great mentor, and I feel honoured to have worked with her. She and the other registered nurse taught me so much about the medical clinic. I will never forget the sincerity of a very special administrative assistant who offered her guidance and wisdom. Even though this employment opportunity ended, I walked away with a wealth of knowledge and experience. Giving 110 percent of myself, I went into work every day and worked extremely hard for this company.

The next few days were tough on me. Negative thoughts kept flooding through my mind: *I am never going to find a job like this one. I have to start all over again. All those interviews where employees focus on the wheelchair and not the person or qualifications they represent—I can't do this anymore.*

The only thing that kept my sanity was a small chalkboard in our kitchen. My home care girls decided to start a countdown with the number of days marked on the calendar until Jeff and I would leave for our honeymoon in St. Lucia. Since I had more time than I knew what to do with, that chalkboard became so important. It read—72 days remaining.

I have had the opportunity to reach out to other disabled individuals around the world who are living with limb-girdle muscular dystrophy. One gentleman living with LGMD from South Africa worked for a corporation for more than ten years. The company expanded its offices and located his office on the second floor. He explained to his employer that it was too difficult to climb stairs to get to his office. They simply did not care. He managed to climb the stairs every day for a year before he had to leave his job. This is not acceptable conduct.

I conversed online with a young woman from the United States who also has LGMD. After attending college for three years, she earned her diploma and graduated. She applied for every position in her skill set. She was interviewed for many of these positions but was never hired. She now collects $400.00 per month in Social Security. At the age of twenty-four, she still has to borrow money from her parents for her basic needs.

My sister worked for a local company for twenty-nine years and was let go because they thought she was a liability. This company refused to offer her benefits because it would be too costly. My sister never asked for benefits. The company was concerned that she would fall at work and sue them. Several personal support workers assisted my sister in the bathroom as well as to and from her car as she entered and exited work. After almost thirty years of great customer service, they terminated her employment and offered her only three weeks of severance. Thankfully, we heard about an excellent litigation lawyer in Hamilton. The company had to compensate my sister a week's wage for each year served as severance pay. These actions by different corporations all over the world are not acceptable. When are these businesses going to be held accountable for their unethical business practices?

While I truly believe that events happen in our lives for a specific reason, the next few months were very difficult for me. Feelings of self-doubt approached me once again. To relieve some of the anxiety, I gave my old job coach a call. Instead of feeling sorry for myself, I decided to be more productive and attend weekly sessions with my employment counsellor. Together, we looked for new employment opportunities. When you fall off the horse, you climb back up on the saddle and ride the horse again.

An old adage states that when one door closes, another one opens. I didn't know where my life was headed, but it was moving forward whether I liked it or not. I heard a profound expression: There is strength in vulnerability. It takes a strong, gutsy person to persevere amid adversity. In order to move forward in my life, I needed to focus on positive aspects of my life. In order to fill the long days that I used to spend working, I continued writing my personal memoir as well as filling out applications to find new employment. Writing my thoughts and feelings on paper was difficult but therapeutic.

Good and bad days were ahead of me. When I felt sad, I looked at that chalkboard. *Wow, only ten more days before we leave on our trip.* We planned our honeymoon at the Sandals Grande in St. Lucia. Boy, did I need a pick-me-up.

Our Honeymoon in St. Lucia

We flew out of Toronto on Christmas Day 2010. This was the first trip Jeff had been on in twenty years and our first big trip together. We both found it difficult leaving our family over the holidays. Five hours later, we landed on the plush tropical island of St. Lucia. The airport crew in St. Lucia were so accommodating. They asked Jeff to help them with my electric wheelchair.

Once I was settled into my chair, we cleared through customs to collect our luggage. We had checked two pieces of luggage and had one carry on with us. We scanned through the luggage. I spotted our large suitcase, but we could not find Jeff's bag. I calmly said to myself, *Don't panic, Shelley. It probably has not been unloaded from the plane.* Oh, how I wished this was the case. After searching for fifteen minutes, it was apparent that Jeff's luggage was nowhere to be found. I thought of all the new dress shirts I had purchased for Jeff to wear at Sandals, since it had a dress code for dinner reservations. We had to file a lost luggage claim at the airport. I was so upset. Jeff seemed to be okay with the news. The airport staff told us not to worry; they would locate it and send it on the next flight. We would have his suitcase by tomorrow.

When we went outside the airport doors, the Sandals' bus had already left for the resort. Since our travel agent told me that my wheelchair would not fit in the bottom of the bus and alternate transportation would need to be arranged, I was not overly worried. The Sandals' agents at the airport called on a gentleman named Bob, who had a private minivan to transport tourists to and from the airport. He arrived at the airport five minutes after the call was placed. Jeff and Bob loaded my wheelchair and our one piece of luggage and off we went.

This was my second time in St. Lucia. I remembered the ride through the mountains. Vehicles drive on the left side of the road, unlike roads in Canada and the United States. The scenery is breathtaking, but these roads are treacherous—especially when there is heavy rainfall. Almost three hours later, we arrived at the resort.

Our first impression of the resort was that it was absolutely beautiful. The open air lobby was grand, with plush furniture, gleaming marble floors, and the most incredible Christmas tree decorated in exquisite ornaments and lit with soft, tiny white lights. Elegant pink, white, and red poinsettias accented the lobby. It was the first Christmas Jeff and I had been away from home, our family, and our little animals. I knew this was going to be the most amazing vacation.

We were escorted to our deluxe ocean view room by a staff member of the concierge. The first thing Jeff and I noticed was the huge pillar-poster king-sized bed. We could spread out on this bed with no Maxwell, Bailey, or Sienna lying on us and disrupting our sleep. We did wonder how Jeff would get me up on the bed because it was so high. The bathroom was fully accessible with a large shower and a raised toilet seat.

The next morning, we walked around the resort. The beach, the pools, and the gardens were simply beautiful—and the sun was hot! On our first morning, Jeff wore jeans and a button-up shirt to breakfast. The guests sitting across the table from us asked Jeff, "Aren't you a little warm in those long pants?" Of course, this started the conversation about our lost luggage. Before the end of the first day, Jeff was officially known as the funny guy from Canada who had no luggage, except for some underwear and two more pairs of pants that I had thrown in my suitcase.

After breakfast, we headed to the hotel souvenir shop to purchase a swimsuit for Jeff. All they had were medium-sized swimsuits, but we could not afford to be too choosy. He didn't even have a pair of shorts to wear. We purchased a dress shirt for him to wear to dinner that evening.

All we could do now was wait to see if our luggage would arrive. We made our way out to the pool just before noon. One of the water sports staff members approached me and said that a gentleman was looking for me. I was a little shocked but remembered that I had spoken to a gentleman named Ken on the Trip Advisor website. I didn't know what country Ken was from, but I remember asking about the accessibility, ramps, etc., at the Sandals Grande St. Lucia. He had visited this resort before and explained to me that the resort was very wheelchair friendly. Some of the ramps were a little steep, but I should be able to access all the amenities of the resort. Ken and his wife, Mira, arrived Christmas Day from England.

I was quite surprised and happy that Ken had sought us out. We hadn't realized Ken was an honorary member of the Sandals Grande because he was such a frequent visitor. We found him to be an amazing person. He was a paying guest like everyone else, but he always went out of his way to help others at the resort. He was quite concerned about Jeff's luggage when it had not arrived by the second day. He spoke to the manager of the resort, who sent three more dress shirts for Jeff to our guest room. We ran into Ken so many times the next day that Jeff and I asked, "Are you stalking us?" Of course, Ken knew that we were joking. Jeff and I met another really nice couple, Rob and Maria, from London, England. They too were on their honeymoon. We sat with them at the pool. Rob, Maria, Ken, Mira, Jeff, and I sat together at the beach party and the Sandals' street party.

Each day by mid-afternoon, the St. Lucian sun was scorching. Jeff helped me into the pool for a refreshing dip. Sometimes he lifted me on to one of the swim-up bar stools. Those frosted fruity drinks were amazing! We all got to know the pool bartenders and what their "special" drinks were. Jeff would carry me out of the pool and over the threshold. I remember one gentleman from the United States saying to us, "Ah, you two are so romantic."

Jeff had to open his mouth and comment, "Thanks, but actually my wife can't walk worth a shit!" He turned to look over in the direction of our lounge chairs and spotted my wheelchair. This poor guy was so embarrassed. Jeff and I started to laugh. I think he realized that Jeff was playing him and didn't need to feel bad about his comment. By the end of the third day on our honeymoon, most people had the honour of meeting Jeff, whether or not they wanted to.

One evening, we were at the lobby bar watching the live entertainment. After a couple of glasses of wine, Jeff wanted me to get up from my chair and slow dance with him. I dared him to come out to the center of the dance floor and sit on my lap as I spun my chair around to the music. He was a little embarrassed but decided to take me up on my offer. Everyone watched us. I think they thought we were a cute couple. After one song, I made Jeff get up and off of my lap. Jeff is only about one hundred sixty pounds, but after one dance he felt like two hundred fifty.

Jeff and Shelley at the main pool

We met so many couples of all ages celebrating their honeymoon just as we were. A woman from Florida sat beside us at the street dance. She was so nice and commented that Jeff and I looked like we were the happiest, most in love couple at the resort. I thanked her and smiled.

Jeff calmly replied, "It appears that way, but I am heavily medicated and my wife drinks a lot." I couldn't believe he'd said that. After spending another ten minutes with Jeff, she realized he was nothing more than a witty smart-ass.

That same evening, Ken and Mira joined us. Ken gave Jeff a taste of his own medicine. Jeff likes to wear lounge pants to sleep in. Unfortunately, all his lounge pants were in his lost luggage. I guess Jeff should not have told Ken earlier that week that he was wearing my snowflake flannel pajama bottoms. I laughed hysterically when Ken announced to our entire table that Jeff had been wearing his wife's sexy snowflake bottoms and that I could not imagine wearing those bottoms ever again.

The week in St. Lucia was half over. I wanted time to stop. We were having so much fun and meeting wonderful people. The weather was incredible, the scenery was breathtaking, the entertainment was great, and the gourmet food was mouthwatering. We had heard that the weather in Canada at the time was very cold. As all flights were canceled, quite a few people from the eastern United States had to stay for a couple extra days. I hoped that Jeff and I could get stranded on this island for a few extra days. The evenings were so peaceful. I loved the soft sounds of the whistling frogs and the waves on the beach.

Jeff and Shelley in the gardens

Days four and five passed with no sight of our luggage. We returned to the Sandals' boutique to purchase Jeff a handsome dress shirt for the New Year's Eve Gala. Jeff headed to the front lobby every day in hopes of news about his luggage. Finally, the airline located his luggage in Toronto; in fact, it had never left. There were flights from Toronto to St Lucia every day. What was the problem?

One evening, Jeff and I walked through the lobby and recognized another couple that we had been introduced to by Ken and Mira. Seamus and Caroline, an elegant couple from England, were shooting a game of pool when we passed by. I thought we would say hello, but before I had the chance, Jeff yelled out, "Nice balls, Seamus!"

Seamus slowly turned, before looking to see who it was and said, "Jeff, I wouldn't expect anything less from you!" All four of us laughed at Seamus's comment. At that moment, I thought, *Shelley, what were you thinking when you agreed to marry this man?*

New Year's Eve at Sandals was truly an extravagant event. Countless workers spent hours setting up for the big night. A platform was built over the main pool area. Round tables were set with floor-length white linen tablecloths. The chairs were covered in long-skirted black and white linens with the backs tied in elegant bows. The women were dressed in glittery gowns. The gentlemen wore dress shirts and ties; some wore tuxes. Ken looked dapper in his black-and-white tuxedo. Mira wore a long black-and-white gown. Jeff wore a beautifully embossed white dress shirt and linen dress pants. I wore a black-and-white polka dot cocktail dress. Maria wore a long black gown, and Rob wore a black-and-white pin-striped shirt with black dress pants. I have never seen a table of guests so colour coordinated.

The theme of the evening was Water, Fire, and Earth. Water buffet tables included fish, lobster, shrimp, clams, and mussels. Barbequed steak, prime rib, chicken, and pork were all part of the Fire theme. Earth incorporated any item of food that was grown from the ground, including vegetables, salads, and grains such as bread and rolls. What an incredible display of food. The champagne was fabulous and was constantly replenished by our white-gloved servers.

After dinner, at around 8:30 p.m., it started to rain. Jeff ran back to the room to get an umbrella in case the rain became heavier. Maria and I were sipping our champagne, giggling, when the light rain turned into a tropical downpour. Rob, Maria's husband, grabbed a waiter's tray and held the tray over me so that I wouldn't get wet. Everyone was running for shelter to stay dry. It seemed like an eternity before Jeff finally returned. He was dressed in a different outfit.

The first thing he uttered from his mouth was, "Guess what just arrived in our room, Shelley—my flipping luggage!" Everyone at our table was in shock.

I was a little embarrassed that Jeff swore in front of everyone. The funny thing was that we were leaving the following afternoon. This was the first time that week that Jeff showed any negative emotion. He was extremely upset. I wittedly commented, "Honey, now you don't have to wear my snowflake bottoms tonight!" Our table of guests laughed.

We arrived at the airport the following afternoon. Jeff jokingly replied, "Shelley, I wonder what they will do to your luggage on the way home!"

"Jeff, please don't joke about something like that," I admonished him. We arrived in Toronto at around 9:30 p.m. after a long five-hour flight. After we cleared customs, Jeff and I went to pick up our luggage. We were pleasantly surprised that our entire luggage arrived in one piece.

This was not the case when we went to pick up my electric wheelchair. It was in several pieces with wires hanging everywhere. A young security guard stopped us and told us that one of the luggage handlers was angry that he had to take extra time to unload the chair to a separate cart. Carelessly, the handler forgot to put on the brakes and raise the bars along the cart. The wheelchair fell four feet off the cart onto the ground and landed on the controller. I don't remember ever seeing Jeff so angry in a public place. At least we had the security guard as a witness. I started to cry when Jeff started to yell, "This wheelchair is my wife's legs; this is her only mode of transportation."

We filed another claim that evening, this time for my electric wheelchair. Two days later, a home health care company from Hamilton picked up my wheelchair and left a rental chair for me to use while they waited for the parts to come in to fix my chair. I wrote a long letter to the travel company, submitting all the receipts for the new clothes we had to buy for Jeff during our stay at the resort. I explained to them that we were especially disappointed with this company and how they put a damper on our honeymoon. Along with the rental wheelchair, they covered the bill for all the parts and service performed on my chair, and they reimbursed us for the clothes. They also offered us a gift voucher for five hundred dollars off our next vacation. Jeff and I were satisfied with this gesture.

For those with disabilities, travelling outside of your local area can be challenging, but it is possible. In Ontario, with the proper documentation, a support person can travel free or at a discounted rate, depending on the mode of transportation. If you live in other areas of Canada or the United States and wish to travel, check the support options that are available to you through local travel services and various nonprofit organizations such as the MDA. They may not be able to assist you, but may guide you in the right direction toward alternate support.

While travelling by plane, your wheelchair needs to be folded and protected to minimize the amount of possible damage. Protect the control panel, remove the foot rests and bungee them to the back rest, and remove the seat cushion. Most airlines will allow you to remain in your own wheelchair until you reach the airplane door. The airline staff will allow you to transfer to one of their chairs to travel to your seat. If the airline damages your wheelchair, they are responsible for replacing it or covering its repair costs. Some people prefer to rent a wheelchair for fear of their vehicle being damaged.

Before booking your trip, ask for a wheelchair-accessible bathroom at the hotel you are staying in. Be specific when inquiring about the hotel room and bathroom. I require a shower stall with grab bars. Some bathrooms state they are accessible, but this may mean grab bars on a regular bathtub setting. Some destinations have home health care agencies nearby where you can rent commodes or Hoyer lifts. Specialty travel agents are available and can take care of your accessible needs while travelling. Visiting other countries is rewarding; never consider that you are unable to travel.

Starting Over

S ince last November, I have applied for eighty jobs and have been interviewed by eight employers. Unfortunately, I have not found employment, but I will never give up. I am extremely optimistic and persistent about finding employment and believe another position will come my way. There will be an unwavering employer who appreciates my qualifications and potential. It takes a strong, tenacious employer to hire a person with physical challenges. In our fast-paced society, companies expect one individual to successfully complete work tasks that years ago took three people to accomplish.

While the Canadian government has mandated that all new buildings be barrier free for those with physical disabilities, people's attitudes toward persons with disabilities need to change. Any individual with a physical, mental, or intellectual disability wants equal opportunities in the workforce.

According to the Canadian Council on Disabilities: Overall, people with disabilities are nearly twice as likely (1.9 times more) to be living in poverty than people without disabilities (22.9% vs. 9.1%).[5]

Some of these statistics attribute to the fact that many disabled individuals collect a disability allowance or pension. I am eligible for a Canada Pension Plan, but the amount I am entitled to will not be enough

---

5   Disabling Poverty and Enabling Citizenship: Understanding the Poverty and Exclusion of Canadians with Disabilities. Council of Canadians with Disabilities. http://www.ccdonline.ca/en/socialpolicy/poverty-citizenship/demographic-profile/understanding-poverty-exclusion.

to cover our household expenses. As an individual living with a disability, I want to make a contribution to society. My six years of postsecondary education should count for something. If given the opportunity, I would love to talk to future employers about disabled people. Education and knowledge are the key components to acceptance and equality of all persons in the workplace.

As of December 2009, the Accessibility of Ontarians Disabilities Act requires all disabled individuals the right to have a barrier-free surrounding for equitable customer service, employment, information, communication, transportation, and built environments. Built environments refer to buildings or other service areas that disabled individuals use such as medical clinics, educational facilities, and shopping malls.

Living with a disability and finding work is difficult. Contact local government agencies or private companies that offer employment services, including interview skills and resume writing to assist in your job search.

For disabled individuals who are not capable of working, support income is available in Canada at the federal and provincial levels of government to help citizens with their financial needs. In Ontario, the Ontario Disability Support Program is an allowance based on income levels for people over the age of eighteen living with a disability. The Canadian Disability Pension Plan is available for those individuals who have made a contribution through employment and can no longer work. This pension is calculated according to the number of years of service employed as well as the amount of yearly gross income earned and contributed. Other countries may offer financial support, which may be identified differently, such as Social Security in the United States. You may also consider volunteering. It will keep you busy and is extremely rewarding to be able to offer your time and support to help others in need.

Jeff and I purchased a cottage in Kingsville, Ontario, in June 2011. This location is very special to us since we celebrated our marriage in this quaint area. We hope to retire and move to the most southern town in Canada in ten years. In the meantime, we plan on spending our summer holidays and every other weekend at the cottage.

As of summer 2011, I remained unemployed; but thankfully, I still collected employment insurance to help with the household finances. I chose to be persistent and remain positive while looking for meaningful employment and, hopefully, that great job will become a reality one day. When and if a disability reaches a point where it is too difficult to work, disability support income is available in Canada to help citizens with their financial needs.

Our new cottage in Kingsville, Ontario

My aunt has her own artisan shop down the road. Until the next employment opportunity occurs, I hope to display some of my watercolour paintings and possibly teach an art workshop. It was extremely warm in southern Ontario this past summer. Jeff and I still find it hard to believe we own a beautiful cottage thirty feet from Lake Erie. Since I am unemployed, we have spent a lot of time at the cottage in Kingsville with our dogs Bailey and Maxwell and our cat, Sienna.

Original Watercolour Mustang by Shelley Tudin

Original Watercolour Cobra by Shelley Tudin

I hired two new personal support workers to assist me during the time I spend in Kingsville. Both of these women were incredibly nice, hardworking, and very reliable; they blended into our family unit. Hilda is very kindhearted, upbeat, and carefree. Brenda is extremely generous, wild natured, and has an incredible sense of humour.

Brenda is experienced in caring for elderly people; however, she never had the opportunity to work with a younger disabled individual. Brenda and I spent a lot of time laughing. She loved my upbeat, bubbly personality and admired my witty character. One evening while assisting me with my pyjamas, she remarked, "Shelley, you are the most courageous person I have ever met. I admire your determination and character. You are a gift from God and a true blessing in my life." Wow, I didn't know how to respond to those admirable comments except to thank her.

One Saturday evening, Brenda decided to stay after her shift. We ordered Chinese takeout and enjoyed laughing and talking for hours after a few glasses of wine. Not surprisingly, I began to feel a little tipsy and my balance was not good. Jeff had to carry me into the washroom, where Brenda and I got the giggles. We laughed so hard my stomach hurt. I loudly blurted out, "Brenda, don't you think I am the coolest *handicrapper* you have ever known?" Brenda laughed louder. Jeff ended up putting me into bed that night because Brenda and I broke into laughter just looking at one another. I am so thankful I have personal support workers at home and at the cottage. Their dedication and assistance allows me to live a productive life despite the daily obstacles I encounter.

Good-bye, My Dear Friend

A couple of weeks prior to Labour Day, I received a letter requesting my presence for jury duty selection. Still unemployed and collecting employment insurance, I decided I had available time and was up for the challenge of jury duty. On September 6, 2011, the jury selection process began. Even though I was not hesitant to accept, it was a nerve-racking process. Two hours later, I was selected as the twelfth juror in a murder case. I immediately thought, *What have I gotten myself into?* The case was scheduled to begin the following day. There was no time to back out now. The court clerk approached me in the jury room. On behalf of the superior court judge, she asked if I was still willing to be a part of this case. I explained to her that I was competent and quite honoured to be a part of this opportunity.

The Superior Court of Justice hears the most serious criminal cases under the criminal code of Canada. The court is composed of the superior court judge, the judge's deputy, the court registrar, the crown prosecutor, the defence counsel, the jury, the accused and witnesses who are called on to testify. I love watching *Dateline* and *48 Hour Mystery*. Even though the events are quite tragic, it is extremely interesting trying to uncover the mystery of who did it with the evidence that is presented. Being a juror on a murder case is nothing like television. The list of witnesses and the large amount of evidence to sort through is a painstaking experience. The witnesses are emotional, and the evidence can be disturbing to hear and see.

After the first three days of trial, I was relieved that the weekend had arrived. My family planned to celebrate my sister, Michele's, birthday that

Saturday. We spent a beautiful day swimming in my mother's pool and enjoying barbecued burgers and salad for dinner. This was the last birthday celebration at our family home on Kensington Avenue. My mother finally decided it was time to sell our family home. The bills and work involved with the upkeep of her home had become too stressful. She had kept the family home for as long as she could and had lived alone the past ten-and-a-half years after my father's death. My mother's memories are tied to this home, forty years of marriage and raising three children. My sister and husband are in the process of having a new accessible home built, which includes a beautiful granny suite on the lower level for my mother. She will have a ravine lookout and walkout entrance.

Our great friend Uncle Buck has always been invited to our family birthday parties and special functions. Once again, he had all of us laughing as we reminisced about his hospital visit the year before. Uncle Buck previously had been diagnosed with diabetes. Unfortunately, an ingrown hair caused a boil on his backside, which became infected and septic. He was admitted into the hospital with a high fever and delirium. Three weeks of antibiotics administered intravenously did not eliminate the infection and blood poisoning. The surgeon rushed Uncle Buck into the operating room to lance the infected area to drain the poison and relieve the pressure that caused him so much pain.

One Sunday afternoon, I visited Uncle Buck in the hospital and brought him a coffee. He was in so much pain that an IV morphine drip had been inserted into his arm. He wanted me to go home so he could be left alone because the pain was so intense. I understood how he felt. I remembered the agony I had been in after I broke my left femur and right hip. Narcotics numb some of the pain, but the medication can upset the stomach. I left him to rest. As I drove down the hospital corridor in my wheelchair I saw my brother and his fiancé heading in my direction with coffee. Buck must have had another dose of morphine because the soreness had abated. He was able to spend some quality time with my brother and his girlfriend. He compared his private areas to two large grapefruits when he opened his hospital gown to show his guests. They burst out laughing.

At the party on that September evening, Uncle Buck demonstrated how he had to walk lugging these two grapefruits around with him. The tears rolled down my face as we all laughed with him. I remember saying, "Uncle Buck, you were lucky to survive that situation; you could have died." Around nine o'clock that evening, we all decided to head home. Uncle Buck had expressed how tired he had been feeling and that he was experiencing a great deal of heartburn. I drove my electric wheelchair down the driveway of my mother's home and became teary eyed when I said to Buck, "In another two months, our family home will be occupied by strangers. I am going to miss this house."

Uncle Buck said to me in his raspy voice, "Shelley, stop that, you know I do not like to see you cry."

Monday, September 12, 2011, started out as any other day except that I was part of a murder trial. After a long day of hearing witnesses and evidence, I arrived home around 5:00 p.m., ate dinner, and got into my pyjamas. Around 10:00 p.m., my sister, Michele, called me on the telephone. The first question she asked was, "Is Jeff home from work yet?"

I replied, "Yes, he's sitting beside me. Why?"

Her voice sounded strange, as though she had been crying. I asked, "Is everything all right, Michele?"

She said, "No, Shelley." My heart began to pound as she started to cry.

I panicked and asked again, "What's wrong, Michele?"

She spoke, "We lost Uncle Buck tonight! The paramedics were at his house and worked on him for more than an hour, but they could not save him. He's dead, Shelley!"

I started screaming, "No, Michele, no; this can't be happening. No, not Uncle Buck, we were just with him on Saturday." I went into shock. I couldn't control the tears and began to cry louder and louder. I asked, "Do Mom and Johnny know?"

Michele was just as upset and answered, "Mom is with Johnny and Deb. They are in shock." None of us could believe the events that had unfolded.

After the phone conversation ended, I cried. Jeff held me tightly as I continued to scream out loud. I cried for four hours before I fell asleep. My eyes were swollen shut when I woke in the morning. My first thought was, *How am I going to function during jury duty today?* I don't know how I managed to pull myself together that morning. My home care worker helped me out of bed to get ready for the day I was about to face.

The other jury members knew something was wrong. I started to cry when I explained, "One of my best friends passed away last night." I tried to pull myself together before I entered the courtroom. It was difficult to concentrate. During the lunch break, one of the court officers spoke to the Superior Court judge about the sudden death of my friend.

I was surprised and touched when he announced in the courtroom to everyone, "It has been brought to my attention that one of your fellow jury members has had a death in the family and is quite distraught. The jury member will need to be present at the funeral at the end of the week. Out of respect, we will not require the jury to be present during that day." A couple of tears rolled down my cheek at the compassion the judge showed toward me.

I cried myself to sleep every night that first week. Each morning and evening, I drove my electric wheelchair to and from the courthouse and my home. Most of those trips were spent thinking about Buck. I know my brother John was devastated by the news. Uncle Buck had worked part time at the printing shop for my brother's boss. Every afternoon, Buck went on a coffee run for the employees. Every evening, Buck was with my brother hanging out or watching the hockey game. The print shop employees were devastated when they heard Buck had died. My brother took the entire week off work to mourn the death of his best friend.

Uncle Buck was acknowledged and highly respected by many people in our city, and hundreds came to pay their respects at the visitation. People stood in line for two hours to reach his casket. What a difficult night. Every friend and relative of the Kormos family attended the visitation. Some drove three hours to Brantford to say good-bye to a cherished man. The funeral was just as difficult. There wasn't a dry eye in the church that morning. John was asked to be an honorary pallbearer even though he could not lift the casket with the other pallbearers.

I felt especially sad for Buck's ninety-nine-year-old mother. Buck adored his dear mother. Fifteen years earlier, Buck had promised his terminally ill father that his mother would never have to live in a nursing home. Prior to the funeral, we discovered why Uncle Buck died so suddenly. Uncle Buck had not been feeling well. That morning, he was with a good friend when he coughed up some pinkish fluid. His friend instructed him to go to the walk-in clinic. Unfortunately, the clinic did not open until 9:00 a.m. Buck made the decision to see his family physician the following day. He worked that afternoon and visited my brother at around 6:00 p.m. Buck then left to purchase a coffee and chat with a couple of his friends before heading home. Lying down in bed around 8:00 p.m., he suddenly ran upstairs to get his mother's attention. He couldn't speak and ran for the sink. He vomited a massive amount of blood; seconds later, he collapsed on the kitchen floor. His dear mother called 911. Buck had suffered a gastric aortic aneurysm; the paramedics who worked on him said he passed on quickly without pain.

A gastric aortic aneurysm refers to a bulge in the vessels near the heart or abdomen. If the bulging stretches the artery too far, this vessel may burst, causing a person to bleed to death. Buck had been tired and complained of heartburn. His doctor had arranged for Buck to have some upcoming tests, but unfortunately he never made it.

I found a verse on the Internet a few weeks after Buck's passing. It explained how I felt after losing my friend. I posted it on the wall of my Facebook page to honour my friend. It read: *If tears could build a stairway, and memories a lane, I'd walk right up to Heaven, Uncle Buck, and bring you home again!*

After four long weeks of hearing all the evidence and listening to the crown prosecutor and the defence counsel, a very important decision had to be made. A victim lost his life and another person was on trial for his murder. As a juror, it is important to weigh all of the evidence and make the correct decision. Someone's life was lost; another person's freedom is in the hands of twelve people. We deliberated for only three hours, finding the defendant guilty of second degree murder. A second degree murder conviction carries a prison sentence up to twenty-five years, one life term, with or without parole. I will never forget this experience.

At the end of September 2011, I applied for a part-time medical receptionist/secretary position at a ministry health clinic. I started to think I was never going to find a job in the medical field. When you least expect something to happen, even though you remain positive, the unexpected happens. My interview went well. I was quite optimistic about landing the job; however, other interviews had been successful and still I had not been hired.

In mid-October 2011, I received a call from the local health clinic where I had interviewed. They offered me a part-time medical secretary/receptionist position. After twelve long months of looking for employment, one tenacious employer allowed me the opportunity to work again. Although this position was part time, the clinic offered me full-time hours until their regular full time staff returned to work.

Change is difficult for me, especially all the anxieties that accompany starting a new job and meeting new people. Once again, I faced the daunting challenge of working with others who had no experience with a disabled individual. During the first six weeks, the stress made it difficult for me to sleep at night and to concentrate at work. I was petrified others would judge me and my abilities to perform simple tasks that my coworkers could perform quickly. Coworkers may judge my ability, intelligence, and character, but I know I work hard and refuse to let others bully or insult me concerning my job performance.

One evening, after a long day at work, I arrived home to the fresh smell of Pine-Sol on our glistening hardwood floors. The house had just been cleaned earlier that day by one of my support workers named Sherry. Another personal support worker, Mary, who met me after work, boosted me up out of my wheelchair and we headed down the hall to my en suite bathroom. After assisting me onto the raised commode, Mary went into the kitchen to start dinner preparations. I started to defecate but thought it odd that I did not hear the water splash in the toilet bowl. My first thought was that I must not have sat far enough back on the seat, so my shit must have hit the front part of the bowl. I started to urinate and suddenly froze as I heard liquid dripping on to the clean floor.

I yelled, "Oh no! Oh no! Mary, I need your help, come quickly."

She ran down the hall in a panic and asked, "What's the matter, Shelley? You scared me to death. I thought you fell off the toilet seat."

I yelled back, "Mary, it's worse than me falling off the seat. My house cleaner forgot to lift the toilet bowl seat lid before she put my commode back over the toilet." Mary seemed confused until I pointed downward, so she could look under the open commode. She finally realized what happened. The toilet lid was closed. Poor Mary cleaned up my smelly deposit as well as a floor covered in urine. I was so embarrassed.

Mary nonchalantly said, "Don't worry about this, Shelley. Do you know how many dirty butts and diapers I clean in a day?"

I replied, "You may clean a lot of crap in a day, but you shouldn't have to clean mine." I didn't know whether to laugh or cry. After apologizing to her at least three times, she replied, "It's a shitty job, but someone has to do it." We both got the giggles. I thought it best to telephone Sherry to explain the importance of keeping the toilet lid open so no more unfortunate accidents happen. Sherry apologized over and over again as Mary was on her hands and knees rewashing the floor. Mary jokingly replied, "Don't ever let this happen again, or I will be forced to come over to your home and injure you!" We all laughed as Mary made the best of this stinky situation.

After several weeks of employment, my nerves had calmed; however, I still wished my body could move faster in order to contribute more to the team of coworkers. It is often difficult for those who do not live with a disability to understand the fatigue and exhaustion that disabled individuals experience while working. In order to live a productive life, I arrange a daily schedule, which is imperative to follow.

My day starts with a 6:00 a.m. arrival and wake-up call from one of my personal support workers. She helps me sit up and lifts me out of bed to a standing position. Using her arms for assistance, I walk to the bathroom to get washed and dressed while sitting on a raised commode chair. Once I am dressed, my support worker lifts me from the commode and walks with me to my dresser where I apply makeup and do my hair without assistance. Since I am unable to raise my arms, it is difficult to style my hair the way I would like to. After the visual presentation is complete and I take my medications, we slowly walk down the hall to the kitchen where I get into my electric wheelchair. I need help putting on my coat and shoes, and then I have a quick, ten-minute breakfast and coffee before a wheelchair transit bus picks me up at my home and transports me to work. At lunch, another support worker, Angie, arrives at my place of employment and lifts me up out of my wheelchair to use the facilities. I met Angie almost five years when she worked for another home care agency called Outreach Attendant Services. As this is the only washroom break I have during the day, I try to limit my intake of fluids.

Around 5:00 p.m., the wheelchair transit bus picks me up at the clinic along with others travelling on the bus as we patiently wait our turn to be delivered to our destination. Upon arrival at home, Dee, my dinner hour home care worker, meets me and lifts me out of my wheelchair. She starts dinner and, depending on how tired I feel, I may assist her with the meal preparation. Once in a standing position, my leg muscles are stiff after a long day sitting on the job. Walking is difficult as I slowly move down the hall to the bathroom. After using the facilities, I struggle to get into shower—a hot shower usually helps limber my stiff muscles. After a thirty-minute shower and a bear hug lift out, Dee dresses me in my pyjamas before dinner. Most evenings, I eat my dinner in bed to keep my legs elevated, which brings down the swelling in my feet. Jeff works until 9:30 p.m., so we do not eat dinner together until the weekend. Dee has worked for me for almost two years. She is extremely hard-working, reliable, and energetic.

Around 8:30 p.m., another home care worker Sherry arrives for my last bathroom break. Sherry has worked for me more than five years, through CCAC and Direct Funding. She has been an angel to me and others who require assistance because of their disability. Around 9:30 p.m., while sitting up in bed, I write or read, watch a little TV, and try to close my eyes around 10:30 p.m. It seems like only an hour of time passes when I hear the alarm going off the following morning. Once again, the daily routines start over.

I am fortunate that my physical impairments are no worse. I know many disabled individuals who are unable to use their hands or cannot talk and rely on support people twenty-four hours a day. Imagine having to rely on another individual to sit, stand, use the washroom, move around your own home, transport you, prepare your meals, and help you back into bed. When you see a disabled person, try to remember what they experience in a day. Appreciate the effort, time, determination, and strength it takes a disabled individual to lead a productive life. I am blessed and adore all my personal support workers. Their support, friendship, and laughter motivate me to live my life with courage and dignity.

I truly believe every life is a gift from God, including mine. I may not be able to walk without assistance, run, jump, dance, or get out of bed unassisted, but I have the ability to inspire and educate others about patience, acceptance, intolerance, and mutual respect toward those living with physical limitations.

Thoughts from the Author

Living with muscular dystrophy is difficult, but I try to live my life regardless of the diagnosis that ultimately led me down a different path. I am a person with feelings, aspirations, and dreams. We all want the same things out of life: to be loved and to find our inner peace and happiness. Throughout my story, it is clear that inner peace and happiness were not traits inherent in me. It was a process that developed slowly as I moved through various events in my life.

Many who live with muscular dystrophy have experienced life-changing events. Some may have been newly diagnosed with a neuromuscular disease. For others, circumstances changed due to a sudden accident. Keep your chin up. Weak muscles or any other type of disability may be visible externally, but the real you is what's inside. When you feel like giving up, remember that something wonderful is waiting for you around the corner. I want to believe that most people possess goodness in their hearts. Unfortunately, our world is far from perfect. We may not be able to change how others feel or think about disabilities, but we are responsible for our own thoughts, actions, and ultimate happiness.

Reach out to support groups[ii] and learn as much as possible about your condition or disease. The Muscular Dystrophy Associations of Canada and the United States have individual websites containing vast amounts of information pertaining to muscular dystrophy. The links are: www.muscle.ca and www.mda.org. I belong to two online support groups: www.inspire.com and www.mymda.mda.org. These websites have thousands of members who live with neuromuscular diseases or have a family member or loved one with muscular dystrophy. Don't be afraid to lean on your family and friends. They are in your life, so utilize them. It's important to remember that anxiety is the flipside of fear. Anxiety will pass. Fear is a state of mind that can entrap you. By facing your fears, you will live a greater and more fulfilling life.

Remember, you are not the only person who has lived with a disability. Focusing solely on positive thoughts will open incredible doors for you and allow you to create better choices. Those optimistic beliefs will eventually lead you to success and contentment.

I read an article on the Internet about a breakthrough in limb-girdle muscular dystrophy. In May 2008, French and German researchers discovered that people with limb-girdle muscular dystrophy are missing a protein called c-FLIP, which the body uses to prevent the loss of muscle tissue. Researchers are focusing on the cellular and molecular systems that are responsible for creating this specific protein. In time, scientists may possibly develop new drugs to stop the muscle deterioration that occurs in people afflicted with limb-girdle muscular dystrophy.

With funding, time, and research, neuromuscular diseases can become disorders of the past. Until then, we can only hope that one day scientists will find a cure for muscular dystrophy. Until this time, we must live our lives with hope and determination because it is the only one we own.

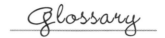

Glossary

colectomy
Refers to the surgical removal or excision of a colon.

colonoscopy
An internal examination using a fiber-optic tube with a camera attached to view the entire intestinal tract or colon.

colostomy
An incision (cut) into the colon (large intestine) to create an artificial opening or stoma to the exterior of the abdomen. This opening serves as a substitute anus through which the intestines can eliminate waste products until the colon can heal or other corrective surgery can be done.

Coumadin
A blood thinner, also called an anticoagulant, used to stop platelets, or heavy cells, from forming clots in the body. It is also known under the brand name of Warfarin.

gastrointestinal endoscopy
A procedure in which a doctor can look inside the lining of the gastrointestinal system with a fiber-optic tube that has a camera attached to it to diagnose gastrointestinal diseases.

peritonitis

The inflammation and secretion of toxins from the abdominal wall of the stomach—due to an infection or the rupture of an organ within the abdomen such as the colon or appendix.

tachycardia

When the heart beats excessively rapidly, the heart pumps less efficiently and provides less blood flow to the rest of the body, including the heart. This rapid heart rate can cause the valve muscle to rupture, resulting in a massive heart attack.

Endnotes

i. For more information on Community Care Access Centres in Ontario for home health care support—http://www.ccac.ca

ii. For Atlantic Canada: Judy Spink, judy.spink@muscle.ca

- For Quebec: Pascale Rousseau, pascale.rousseau@muscle.ca
- For Ontario and Nunavut: Margaret Otter, marg.otter@muscle.ca
- For Western Canada: Maggie Kissel, maggie.kissel@muscle.ca